The Owl and the Nightingale: The Poem and its Critics

KATHRYN HUME is a member of the Department of English at Cornell University.

The Owl and the Nightingale is clearly one of the few major Middle English poems. Despite the clarity and simplicity of its text, however, the poem has occasioned bitter and still unresolved interpretative controversy. Is the key to its meaning to be found in bird lore? the debate form? Is the poem a political or religious allegory? Despite the radical contradictions in the conclusions of previous critics, most of them have implicitly claimed a unique and exclusive validity.

Kathryn Hume's purpose in writing this book is to offer a new account of the poem, one based on a systematic attempt to assess the validity and usefulness of various possible approaches to the work. She shows saneness, balance, and humour both in her criticism of previous interpretations and in her own conclusions. We need, she insists, to understand the nature of the poem before we erect elaborate theories about its meaning.

The contradictoriness of the relevant avian traditions, the birds' complete incompetence as debaters, the poem's curiously indeterminate ending, and the critics' inability to agree even on the subject of the controversy, she argues, make it difficult to see the work as a serious debate about anything. Attempts to find an extrinsic or allegorical meaning have proven radically contradictory and have all neglected large portions of the poem. But since no serious issue is present in the birds' dialogue, the meaning of the poem must indeed be sought elsewhere.

Analysis of *The Owl and the Nightingale*'s sequential impact and its manipulation of audience response emphasize the debate's lack of direction, its bitterness, and also – from the reader's point of view – its humour. Kathryn Hume argues that a great deal is clarified and made comprehensible if we regard the poem as a burlesque-satire on human contentiousness. The birds' illogic, the wandering arguments, the unsystematic introduction of various human concerns, and the inconclusive ending are all consistent with the idea that the poem was written as a witty caricature of petty but vicious human quarrelling.

Both for its sane reinterpretation of what is widely considered one of the masterpieces of Middle English literature and for the interpretative methodology it employs, *The Owl and the Nightingale*: The Poem and its Critics should be of lasting value to medievalists.

KATHRYN HUME

the owl and the nightingale

the poem and its critics

UNIVERSITY OF TORONTO PRESS
TORONTO AND BUFFALO

© University of Toronto Press 1975
Toronto and Buffalo
Printed in Canada

The cover design is based on a misericord in Norwich Cathedral, England.

Library of Congress Cataloging in Publication Data

Hume, Kathryn, 1945–
    The owl and the nightingale.
    Includes bibliographical references and indexes.
    1. The owl and the nightingale.   I. Title.
    PR2109.073H84   1975   821'.1   75–1452
    ISBN 0–8020–5316–5

For Criseyde and Alisoun
enthusiastic birdwatchers

contents

texts and Bibliographies

Two manuscripts of the poem are extant: the preferred, C, is British
Museum MS Cotton Caligula A. ix; the other, J, is Jesus College, Oxford,
MS 29. Both have been edited by J.W.H. Atkins in *The Owl and the
Nightingale* (Cambridge, England: Cambridge University Press 1922),
and are available in facsimile with an introduction by N.R. Ker, EETS
o.s. 251 (London: Oxford University Press 1963). I quote however from
Eric Gerald Stanley's edition of the C text, *The Owl and the Nightingale*
(orig London: Thomas Nelson and Sons 1960; reissued in 1972 by Manchester University Press as part of the Old and Middle English Texts
series). That edition is readily available, excellently edited, and inexpen-
sive, and therefore judged preferable for the convenience of readers of
this book. I am grateful to the Manchester University Press for permission to quote this text.

The recent publication of two reference books makes a separate bibliography here superfluous. For very full checklists of scholarship on
the poem, readers should consult either *A Manual of the Writings in
Middle English: 1050–1500*, general editor Albert E. Hartung, vol. 3
(New Haven: Connecticut Academy of Arts and Sciences 1972), or vol-
ume 1 of *The New Cambridge Bibliography of English Literature*, edited
by George Watson (Cambridge: Cambridge University Press 1974).

preface

The Owl and the Nightingale clearly belongs among the handful of major Middle English poems. Indeed, its cheerful vigour and cockeyed squabbles make it perhaps the most delightful of them. Scholars have long debated its sources, date, authorship, and dialect; more recently, interpretative matters have begun to attract attention. But despite the simplicity of the text, critics' interpretations have proved astonishingly contradictory, and we now find ourselves in an absurd position: half a dozen major readings (and many variants) exist, but although most of them are mutually exclusive, their sponsors have made no attempt either to rebut previous work or to reconcile it with their own. Consequently, the poem, a mysterious planet, is now circled by a number of satellite interpretations, most of them implicitly claiming unique validity.

This book is built on the premise that valid interpretation is possible.[1] The alternative is relativism and the admission that no interpretation is demonstrably superior to any other. Few medievalists, I think, would consciously adopt such a position, and yet in effect this is what students of The Owl and the Nightingale have done. The results are chaotic and self-defeating: each critic who ignores readings contradicting his own is in turn ignored, and criticism of the poem has degenerated into a meaningless game. The first duty of a serious critic in such a situation (and there are others like it in Middle English literature) must be to investigate the nature of the work at issue, and to assess the usefulness of the various approaches which have been or could be made to it. Then and only then is there any point to offering yet another reading – and when the critic does so, he must try to demonstrate its superiority to its predecessors.

My principal object in this book is to discover what is and what is not valid and useful in explaining the form and import of the poem – and then to apply what has been learned. After Chapter 1 (a brief survey of the problems of text, date, and authorship besetting the work), I propose to proceed with an examination of the various ways in which the poem has been approached, starting with the factual and intrinsic, and moving to the allegorical and extrinsic. Chapter 2 tests the viability of bird lore and the avian nature of the protagonists as bases for reading the work. Chapter 3 is a consideration of the importance of the debate form to any interpretation. Chapters 4 and 5 range farther afield to possible referential contexts. Many critics have found the poem meaningless in itself, and so have sought extrinsic frames of reference, treating it as intellectual, religious, or political allegory. My hope here is to see both whether such a procedure has yielded useful insights in the past, and whether we should try to employ it further. My conclusion is that such 'external' readings have not been satisfactory, and probably cannot be made so. Chapter 6 is an attempt to return to the work itself. By analysing its sequential impact in light of our findings about its avian details and debate form, I think we can reach some useful conclusions from internal evidence about the poem's 'formal intention.' In Chapter 7 I draw on my methodological critique to present a case for reading the poem as a burlesque-satire, and in the final chapter this approach is submitted to the same rigorous strictures applied earlier to other readings.

Much of this book is intended to serve as a prolegomenon to future critical study of *The Owl and the Nightingale.* Until some fundamental questions have been answered, there is little object to more new readings. Whether or not the reader accepts my own account of the poem in Chapter 7, I hope that my attempt to clear the field will prove useful: specious readings dependent on flawed logic need to be recognized and discarded, and methodological principles devised to help safeguard future interpretations against the problems and contradictions which have plagued those of the past. If I have succeeded in my aims, future critics will have a fresh base to work from, and will be able legitimately to ignore the many studies based on faulty premises. To date, no agreement has been reached on the most basic points: if they really cannot be settled, then all study will be in vain. At present, critics variously see *The Owl and the Nightingale* as a serious debate (whose theme they cannot agree upon), a *jeu d'esprit* bird poem, a religious allegory, a literary allegory, or a political allegory. My hope is to determine just what kind of poem we are trying to study, and what it is about.

NOTE

1 See E.D. Hirsch, Jr, *Validity in Interpretation* (New Haven: Yale University Press 1967) for a discussion of the hermeneutical problems involved.

acknowledgments

My thanks for helpful advice and criticism are due to R.M. Lumiansky, James L. Rosier, and my husband, Robert D. Hume.

Publication of this book was made possible by grants to University of Toronto Press from the Hull Memorial Publication Fund of Cornell University and from the Andrew W. Mellon Foundation.

THE OWL AND THE NIGHTINGALE: **THE POEM AND ITS CRITICS**

1

some problems of text, date, authorship, and interpretation

Despite intensive study of *The Owl and the Nightingale* over the last sixty years, scholars agree on little beyond its being a Middle English poem about 1800 lines long preserved in two manuscripts.[1] Such an impasse is surprising for there are no significant *lacunae*, and the text offers few difficulties when taken line by line. Yet not only are such interpretative issues as the moral standing of the birds, the subject of their debate, and its outcome undecided, but there is no agreement on purely factual problems such as date of composition, identity of author, or even the palaeographic dating of one manuscript. Perhaps the most peculiar circumstance of all those attending the poem is the utter failure of critics to take this diversity into account. Most recent interpretations are diametrically opposed to some prior attempt, yet not one demonstrates the insufficiency of the alternative. This is a radically unstable state of affairs for if any one of the interpretations can be proven valid, the others will have to be discarded.

My first step in determining why previous critics have failed to establish any certainties will be a brief survey of the problems which beset the poem. This sketch is not meant to be an exhaustive study; for that, one can turn to the introductions by J.W.H. Atkins and E.G. Stanley to their respective editions.[2] This chapter should merely remind the reader of the traditional scholarly cruces of manuscript, author, and date, and of the critical questions concerning the nature of the birds' debate.

With only two manuscripts, whose variants are negligible from an interpretative viewpoint, we might expect that textual matters would be pretty well under control. And indeed, I doubt that our grasp of the poem would be measurably improved were the author himself to explicate such a crux as 'Ne roȝte he þeȝ flockes were / Imeind bi toppes & bi here' (427–8). We have no surety on the descent of manuscripts, but Wells is probably correct in supposing C and J to have had a common original, itself at least one remove from the author's own version.[3] Dating the poem might be easier if our information on this point were precise, but we cannot call this a crucial uncertainty.

The important problem is the palaeographic dating of the C text. Until 1963, all but a very few scholars agreed that C was written in the first half of the thirteenth century, an estimate circumstantially supported by the presence in that manuscript of a chronicle ending in 1216. Lofty arguments for dating the poem have been erected on the foundation of this supposed C text date, for *if* the manuscript was copied in the first half of the century, the reference to 'king Henri' (1091), usually understood to imply his recent death, *must* refer to Henry II (d. 1189) rather than Henry III (d. 1272). Few recent critics have been as judicious as Wells, who was careful to acknowledge (p. xxv) that his argument for the poem's date 'rests ... on the supposed date of the extant manuscripts, especially of C.' This dating of C, and all the interpretative arguments based upon it are called in doubt by N.R. Ker, who flatly asserts:

> In fact, it is not possible to say that one manuscript is earlier than the other. Both seem to have been written in the second half of the thirteenth century. This date is the generally accepted date for Jesus and was the date assigned to ff. 195–261 of Cotton by Sir Frederic Madden. Later writers, except Wright, have placed Cotton in the first half of the thirteenth century. Wright's dating 'probably a little after A.D. 1250' seems to me on the early side. The difference between the hands is a difference of kind, not of date.[4]

Ker should know if anyone does how best to date this manuscript. If he is correct, the poem could have been written eighty or so years later than is usually supposed, in a milieu totally different from that assumed by most critics. New uncertainties are thus introduced into our speculations as one standard assumption proves questionable.

Difficult though it may be to establish facts through the manuscripts, it is harder still to find any certainties concerning the author, his reason

for composing, and the date of composition.[5] For a medieval poem to
be written anonymously is not unusual – indeed it is normal. But the
birds ostentatiously mention one Nicholas of Guildford, and many scholars take this as an indication that he is the author. Another possible candidate is John of Guildford. An early owner of the J text transcribed a
leaf now lost from it containing the following lines:

Mayster Iohan eu greteþ. of Guldeuorde þo.
And sendeþ eu to Seggen. þat synge nul he no.
Ac on þisse wise he wille endy his song:
God Louerd of Heuene. beo vs alle among.
    AMEN.

                                (Stanley, p. 4)

John's claim to authorship has gained little following, for there is no reason to think that these lines apply to this one piece in the compilation,
but it has in its favour the fact that John is apparently a poet, whereas
Nicholas is praised by the birds as a judge. However as Stanley notes
(p. 20), 'The metre of the prayer is not that of O & N, and the pitiful
rhyme þo/no (where þo exists merely to supply a rhyme for no) is
feebler than any in O & N.' Conceivably the poem was composed by
some anonymous friend of Nicholas of Guildford who wished to help
him win preferment; but if so Nicholas had an extraordinarily generous
friend, for both the quality of the poem and its length presuppose a great
deal of hard work. Most scholars are content to treat *The Owl and the
Nightingale* as a plea for advancement written by Nicholas himself, accepting the possibility that he was either conceited or whimsical. The
question of authorship has been much discussed because sound interpretation of the poem may well depend on our understanding the curious
relationship between the narrative voice and the object of its seemingly
exaggerated praise.

    The poem's date is probably the most hotly disputed of the tradi-
tional cruces, and one might well wonder why interest in it should be
so much stronger than the usual scholarly desire for certainty. The reasons are partly psychological, and related to the other enigmatic qualities
of the work. There are many details which seem to have specific historical

referents, and we find frustrating our inability to solve at least the riddle of the date when there is such a wealth of clues. And, of course, a firm date might provide the key which would open up the interpretation. The details which beg for identification are as follows.

The allusion to the king is in lines 1091–2:

Þat underyat þe king Henri –
Iesus his soule do merci! –

This has been read as a reference to (1) Henry II while yet living (by Kathryn Huganir and Henry Barrett Hinckley); (2) Henry II just recently deceased and Henry III not yet ascended (most recent critics); (3) the 'young king' as Henry II's son Henry was called, shortly after *his* death in 1183 (S.R.T.O. d'Ardenne); (4) Henry III (Ten Brink, Morris, Skeat); or (5) Henry III recently deceased (Madden, Hazlitt).[6] Most critics feel that 'Iesus his soule do merci!' is a pious wish for a dead man's soul, but a few have argued that it could be said of the living. Those who think it refers to Henry II after his death date the poem 1189–1216, claiming that, after Henry III's coronation, Henry II would have been distinguished with some epithet like 'the old king' to differentiate him from the reigning sovereign. In any case the phrase is useless for precise dating; Lillian de la Torre Bueno has rightly pointed out that a poet writing before 1189 might have put something like 'Jesus ʒif him grace and merci!' or 'Jesus ʒif him graunt merci!' and the scribe of the source of C and J might have changed the line to its present wording after Henry's death.[7] Such scribal changes in the form of a blessing to reflect their object's death are a well-documented custom. Consequently this crux is a bad foundation for any theory of dating.

Two other passages containing possibly datable evidence are lines 907–10 and 995–1020. In these are mentioned the barbarity of such northern peoples as the inhabitants of Ireland, Scotland, Norway, and Galloway, and a good man from Rome who tried to bring civilized practices to the North. The usual candidates for the man from Rome are Nicholas Breakspear, an Englishman who became Pope Adrian IV (1154–9) and was famous for his work in Norway (Frederick Tupper); Cardinal Vivian, whose embassy to some of these countries started in 1176 (most recent critics); and John the Archchanter, who came to England in 680 to teach Gregorian chanting to the newly established English Church (Bertram Colgrave).[8] Attempts to place the poem by its relation to these and other legatine activities have proved fruitless; legations can be found to support the disparate theories, but by themselves they settle nothing.

There are several contenders for the title of Nicholas of Guildford. Kathryn Huganir (pp. 164 ff.) has argued for Nicholas *filius Thoraldi*, a justice on the southern circuit who would indeed have needed preferment once the papal decree of 1179 barred clerics from secular jobs. Nicholaus *capellanus archidiaconi* (witness to a document of 1209) and Nicholaus *submonitor capituli de Gudeford* (mentioned in 1220, possibly the same man) have had their supporters. Nicholas, Archdeacon of London, has been added to the roster by Anne W. Baldwin, since he was a follower of Gilbert Foliot.[9] And J.C. Russell argues that the candidate for preferment was Nicholas de Aquila, a canon lawyer from near Guildford who may have been the Oxford professor of law named Nicholas mentioned towards the end of the twelfth century.[10] As with the good man from Rome and the possible Henries, too many solutions present themselves for the reference by itself to be decisive.

The word 'foliot' in 'Ne singe ih hom no foliot' (868) has been probed as a possible clue. It appears as a common noun nowhere else in English, but seems from the context to mean 'foolishness.' It may however be a sarcastic pun on the name of Gilbert Foliot, Bishop of London, who was one of the few major clergymen to side with Henry against Becket. Gilbert died in 1187, and Hinckley and Huganir have argued that such a pun is unlikely to have been composed after his death, a logical supposition but not certain enough to date the poem precisely.

Another phrase which looks datable is the Wren's 'þis pes' in

---

Hwat! wulle ȝe þis pes tobreke,
An do þan [kinge] swuch schame?
Ȝe! nis he nouþer ded ne lame.

(1730-2)

Even if the defective metre of line 1731 is not emended (though most editors agree to insert 'kinge'), the passage seems to refer to some specific period of peace. Kathryn Huganir insists that the peace can be none other than the reign of Henry II, lion of justice. Frederick Tupper suggests the peace declared with the Edict of 1195, by which Justiciar Hubert Walter compelled all men over fifteen years of age to take an oath that they would preserve the King's peace, and that 'ded ne lame' means 'dead or infirm,' which could apply to Richard I's health at that time. Anne W. Baldwin argues that the peace is the one established between Henry II and the Church after Becket's death had been atoned for. She equates 'ded ne lame' with Henry's illness following his open-air penance at Becket's tomb in 1174 and his being kicked by a horse in July of the same year. It would not be difficult to discover other 'peaces' to support other dates.

Minutiae have been sifted with grim thoroughness for use in dating. A verbal threat uttered by the angry Owl (150–3) was taken by Atkins (p. 15) as a challenge to judicial combat, and he suggests that this provides a *terminus ad quem* because judicial combat was banned in 1219. But the passage may not be a formal challenge, and furthermore trial by combat was legal under some circumstances until 1819. It was trial by water or fire which was banned.[11] The harshness of the king's sentence on the knight who tried to molest a nightingale (1100–1) may refer to the sort of sentences handed out under Henry II's forest laws.[12] Some of the author's lines seem to reflect knowledge of Marie de France's *Laustic* and Alexander Neckam's *De Naturis Rerum*, but neither work is datable precisely, so the similarities are no help. A.C. Cawley has used other details from the birds' exchanges to argue that the conflict reflects interest in an astrological conjunction of 1186.[13]

We must remember that most of these theories are based on the assumption that the King Henry referred to cannot be Henry III because of the early date of the C text, so none of these critics has looked for events in the third quarter of the thirteenth century which might be relevant to the poem. Scholars may indeed conclude that the date lies somewhere between 1170 and 1216, but present acceptance of various dates within that span rests on faulty premises, and there is room for more work to be done in this area.

When we move from issues subject to scholarly research to those of critical interpretation, matters are hardly improved. There is no agreement on the nature of the opponents: is one right and the other wrong, are both flawed, or are they somehow mutually complementary? Are we meant to be able to judge the debate and award victory, or is it meant to be indeterminable? Just what are the issues at stake? Are there many, or is there one overall issue? And finally why was the poem written?

Critical assessments of the debaters box the compass. J.W.H. Atkins offers a clear statement of the view most attractive to modern taste:

> it is the Nightingale who in the end seems to get the better of the argument ... the Nightingale figures as plaintiff in the law-suit: she is out to remedy an abuse, to right a wrong, and to claim for love-poetry its release from the heavy hand of tradition. Then, too ... the Nightingale is represented on the whole as the better-tempered of the two combatants: she is the more attractive personality, she shows more self-restraint than the Owl, and she indulges to a lesser extent in vile personalities and abuse. And in the end it is the Night-ingale who is made to triumph ... Indirectly, therefore, the poet may be said to have given his verdict.
>
> (pp. lviii–lix)

Atkins's analysis of the issue at stake is his own, but in his attitude toward the Nightingale's character he is typical of Nightingale supporters. Most modern readers would like to agree with Atkins on the relative merit of the birds, for when they allow their own taste to guide them it is the Nightingale who pleases. She is associated with spring and joyful music, with sensual pleasures, and perhaps with love poetry. The Owl, on the other hand, suggests darkness, winter, bad fortune, didactic religious poetry, and an ascetic view of life and sensual pleasures. Those who discount their personal taste and let their carefully cultivated sense of historical perspective guide them will often grant the palm to the Owl on the theory that medieval men would have found the Owl's virtues more pleasing than we do, but there often lurks in their faint praise the suggestion that the Nightingale, though 'wrong,' is attractive whereas the Owl, however 'right,' is repulsive. Hence a characteristic judicious-ness of tone, as the critic tries to be fair.

> No doubt the nightingale is the more likeable character, but there is no denying the shrewdness and tenacity of the owl. Although the author holds the scales evenly balanced between the two the owl seems, on the whole, to get the better of the argument, though

the quicker wit of the nightingale is able to seize on a technical mis-pleading and to claim the victory.[14]

It is the old conflict between beauty, brilliancy, youth, cheerfulness, and a serious, gloomy, sullen old age, between pleasure and asceticism. *Singularly enough*, the poet seems to side with the owl, notwithstanding his very impersonal attitude.[15]

At the beginning of *The Owl and the Nightingale* it is the Nightingale, with its associations with summer and young love, that seems the most attractive of the two birds, but gradually we come to see that the poet is on the side of the moralizing Owl.[16]

The evidence of the poet's supposed preference for the Owl appears when the Nightingale is said to feel hard pressed by the Owl's charges in phrases such as these:

Þe Niȝtingale in hire þoȝte
Athold al þis, & longe þoȝte
Wat ho þarafter miȝte segge;
Vor ho ne miȝte noȝt alegge
Þat þe Hule hadde hire ised,
Vor he spac boþe riȝt an red.

(391–6)

---

or

An hit is suþe strong to fiȝte
Aȝen soþ & aȝen riȝte.

(667–8)

Recently two other interpretations have gained popularity, one arguing for the equality of the two birds, the other for a wholeheartedly positive response to the Owl. Such Owl-supporters are generally of the 'historical criticism' persuasion, and their robust belief in official medieval morality permits them to accept without modern reservations what they consider the 'medieval' reading of the poem. Douglas L. Peterson has expressed this view most forcefully:

> Pedagogically, it [the poem] is a dialectical exercise in which two irreconcilable attitudes toward human experience – the one, essentially traditional and Christian, and the other, sensual and heretical – are represented respectively by a logician in quest of truth and a rhetorician in quest of sophistical victory ... If Nicholas is being presented for preferment to his ecclesiastical superiors, either by a friend or by himself, certainly he has not been placed in the rôle of judge to decide against the logician and defender of The Faith in favor of the sophistical rhetorician who involves herself in open contradiction and who identifies eternal happiness with physical pleasure.[17]

Whether a critic supports the Owl (enthusiastically or reluctantly) or the Nightingale depends on (1) whether he believes that the Owl is superior morally; (2) whether he thinks medieval listeners responded to literature in strict accord with moral truisms; and (3) whether he agrees with the choice of evidence presented to support an interpretation, for the birds' dispute goes in so many directions and is so open to differing constructions that most readings are based on an extremely selective array of details.

The school of thought which insists on the birds' equality is divided; some critics believe the birds to be equal in the sense that they are mutually complementary (Wells, Kincaid), others that they are equally flawed (Kinneavy, Schleusener, Gardner, Hieatt). Yet others, while granting probable equality, are less concerned with the birds' moral worth than with our response to them, claiming we are not meant to take sides (Gottschalk, Lumiansky). And indeed Constance Hieatt, Jay Schleusener, and John Gardner all insist that we are silly to take the poem seriously as a debate. Neither bird is logical, neither has any real point to make; the clash is just dispute for dispute's sake. We should laugh at the squabble, not treat it as a solemn moral conflict.[18]

As for what the poem means – take your choice. It is one humane mind's expression of his love of life (Wells); it is an argument over styles of preaching (Owst), poetry (Atkins, Allen[19]), or singing (Colgrave); it is one of the flurry of works concerned with the planetary conjunction of 1186 and a debate on the validity of astrology (Cawley); it is one of the flurry of pieces written on the Becket controversy and a satire on the distribution of benefices (Baldwin); it is a plea for preferment (Atkins, Huganir, Lumiansky, and others) addressed to a patron – an unknown ecclesiastical superior, Henry II, or Geoffrey, Archbishop-elect of York; it is a moral exhortation (Gottschalk and, to some extent, Robertson and Peterson); it is based on the interplay of diverse traditions related to the two birds (Donovan, Iser).[20] Most of these explanations are mutually exclusive.

Such are the gaps in our picture of the poem. In plain terms we do not know what sort of a poem we are dealing with, what its object is (whether open or allegorically disguised), nor how the audience was supposed to respond. The net result of considerable labour has been close to nil even in matters like dating which are normally susceptible to scholarly assault. To fuel our frustration, the narrative is simplicity itself, having the air of being easy to understand. Yet it has proved far otherwise.

This survey should make plain my reasons for thinking some stock-taking necessary. Interesting though it might be to present a 'new reading' right off, such impetuosity would be ill-advised. Various approaches, all of them plausible and seriously argued, have produced wildly diverse answers to the poem's problems. Without a better understanding of why critical methods have failed, why they are apparently invalid (wholly or in part), one cannot hope to make any real progress. The next four chapters of this study are intended as a prolegomenon to future examination of the poem. Only when the problems of approach are worked out can anyone hope to construct an interpretation with a better theoretical foundation than those already offered.

NOTES

1 Titchfield Abbey may have owned a third, for its medieval library catalogue lists an anthology including 'De conflictu inter philomenam et bubonem in anglicis.' R.M. Wilson discusses this lost manuscript in 'The Medieval Library of Titchfield Abbey' *Proceedings of the Leeds Philosophical and Literary Society* 5 (1938–43) 150–77, 252–76, especially p. 159, and in 'More Lost Literature II' *Leeds Studies in English* 6 (1937) 30–49, especially pp. 31–2. In addition, the Abbey catalogue lists 'Altercaciones inter bubonem et philomenam' among the books 'in gallico.'

2 J.W.H. Atkins, ed. *The Owl and the Nightingale* (Cambridge, England: Cambridge University Press 1922) xi–lxxiii, and Eric Gerald Stanley, ed. *The Owl and the Nightingale* (London: Thomas Nelson and Sons 1960; reprint, Manchester University Press 1972) 17–33, hereafter cited as Atkins and Stanley

3 John Edwin Wells, in the introduction to his edition of *The Owl and the Nightingale* (Boston, Mass.: D.C. Heath 1907, vii–xvii) presents the evidence for this hypothesis. Hereafter cited as Wells

4 *The Owl and the Nightingale*, EETS o.s. 251 (London: Oxford University Press 1963) ix

5 Even the original dialect of the poem is uncertain, though Bertil Sundby argues for Surrey in *The Dialect and Provenance of the Middle English Poem* The Owl and the Nightingale: *A Linguistic Study*, Lund Studies in English 18 (Lund: Gleerup 1950).

6 Nineteenth century scholars' views on the date are discussed in Atkins's introduction, p. xxxiv; Kathryn Huganir explores dating problems at length in *The Owl and the Nightingale: Sources, Date, Author* (1931; reprint, New York: Haskell House 1966) 63–139 (hereafter Huganir), and in 'Further Notes on the Date of *The Owl and the Nightingale*' *Anglia* 63 (1939) 113–34. Henry Barrett Hinckley has taken up the dating problem in 'The Date of *The Owl and the Nightingale*' *MP* 17 (September 1919) 63–74; in 'The Date, Author, and Sources of the *Owl and the Nightingale*' *PMLA* 44 (1929) 329–59; and 'The Date of *The Owl and the Nightingale*: Vivian's Legation' *PQ* 12 (1933) 339–49. S.R.T.O. d'Ardenne identifies the king as the 'young king' in '"Ine so gode kinges londe"' *ES* 30 (1949) 157–64.

7 Lillian de la Torre Bueno, 'A Note on the Date of *The Owl and the Nightingale*' *Anglia* 58 (1934) 122–30

8 See Frederick Tupper, 'The Date and Historical Background of *The Owl and the Nightingale*' *PMLA* 49 (1934) 406–27; Huganir, pp. 63–139; and Bertram Colgrave, '*The Owl and the Nightingale* and the "Good Man from Rome"' *ELN* 4 (1966) 1–4.

9 Anne W. Baldwin, 'Henry II and *The Owl and the Nightingale*' *JEGP* 66 (1967) 207–29

10 J.C. Russell, 'The Patrons of *The Owl and the Nightingale*' *PQ* 48 (1969) 178–85

11 See Sir Frederick Pollock and Frederic William Maitland, *The History of English Law before the Time of Edward I*, 2nd ed. 2 vols. (Cambridge, England: Cambridge University Press 1898) II 599, 632, and George Neilson, *Trial by Combat* (New York: Macmillan 1891) 68–73.

12 Hinckley, in *PMLA* (1929), especially on pp. 338–9, looks to the forest laws. Huganir though, in 'Equine Quartering in *The Owl and the Nightingale*' *PMLA* 52 (1937) 935–45, has argued that the harshness is attributable to the knight's having usurped royal prerogative in decreeing a punishment reserved for treason against the king.

13 A.C. Cawley, 'Astrology in "The Owl and the Nightingale"' *MLR* 46 (1951) 161–74

14 R.M. Wilson, *Early Middle English Literature*, 3rd ed. (London: Methuen 1968) 164

15 Bernhard Ten Brink, *Early English Literature (to Wiclif)*, trans. Horace M. Kennedy (New York: Henry Holt 1883) 215 (italics added)

16 A.C. Spearing, *Criticism and Medieval Poetry* (London: Edward Arnold 1964) 66

17 Douglas L. Peterson, '*The Owl and the Nightingale* and Christian Dialectic' *JEGP* 55 (1956) 13–26; quotation from p. 26. See also D.W. Robertson, Jr 'Historical Criticism' in *English Institute Essays 1950*, ed. Alan S. Downer (1951; reprint, New York: AMS Press 1965) 3–31, especially pp. 23–6.

18 The ideas of the critics mentioned may be found in the following works: Suzanne Moss Kincaid, 'The Art of *The Owl and the Nightingale*' Diss. Western Reserve University 1966; Gerald B. Kinneavy, 'Fortune, Providence and the Owl' *SP* 64 (1967) 655–64, especially p. 664; Jay Schleusener, '*The Owl and the Nightingale*: A Matter of Judgment' *MP* 70 (1973) 185–9; John Gardner, '*The Owl and the Nightingale*: A Burlesque' *PLL* 2 (1966) 3–12; Constance Hieatt, 'The Subject of the Mock-Debate Between the Owl and the Nightingale' *SN* 40 (1968) 155–60; Jane Gottschalk, '*The Owl and the Nightingale*: Lay Preachers to a Lay Audience' *PQ* 45 (1966) 657–67, especially pp. 662–3; and R.M. Lumiansky, 'Concerning *The Owl and the Nightingale*' *PQ* 32 (1953) 411–17, especially p. 414.

19 Richard E. Allen, in 'The Voices of *The Owl and the Nightingale*' *Studies in Medieval Culture* 3 (1970) 52–8, has suggested that one incidental stance in the argument is epic (Owl) against romance (Nightingale).

20 Mortimer J. Donovan, 'The Owl as Religious Altruist in *The Owl and the Nightingale*' *MS* 18 (1956) 207–14; Wolfgang Iser, 'The Owl and the Nightingale: Versuch einer formgeschichtlichen Ortsbestimmung' *Deutsche Vierteljahrsschrift für Literaturwissenschaft und Geistesgeschichte* 33 (1959) 309–23. G.R. Owst's views on the poem are expressed in *Literature and Pulpit in Medieval England*, 2nd ed. (Oxford: Basil Blackwell 1961) 22.

the avian nature
of the protagonists

Because the protagonists are birds, some critics have hoped, logically
enough, that medieval bird lore would furnish the key to this poem; and
indeed their discoveries do help us to understand a few of the turns the
debate takes, as well as various accusations and insults the birds exchange.
Unfortunately those who have built general interpretations upon lore
have arrived at absolutely contradictory conclusions, and neither the interpretations' sponsors nor subsequent writers have recognized what went
wrong. Yet the reasons for divergence are not difficult to understand, and
offer as good a starting point as any for assessment of critical methodology. Nor have all the fruits of this field been garnered; enough remain to
make an investigation of lore worthwhile in its own right. Moreover, critics have virtually ignored a vital question: *why* are birds employed as
the protagonists? A convincing answer to this question might shed light
on the essential nature of the poem. In this chapter therefore I shall first
explore folk, literary, and religious traditions about owls and nightingales,
and then consider the possibility of illuminating the poem by juxtaposing
it to other works with animal principals. These two proceedings should
both clarify the uses and limitations of bird lore for reading the poem,
and help us see how the poem functions. Both too will make us aware of
the poem's astonishingly rich satiric potentialities.

Unlike some of the religious lore I shall consider later in this chapter, the
principal folk traditions are both readily accessible to the modern reader
and indisputably relevant to the poem. Owls are birds of ill omen, associated with darkness and cold, disaster, and death. This dread reputation
stems from their being nocturnal (which strikes men as unnatural and

sinister), from their mournful sounding hoots, and from the hatred other birds display by mobbing owls. That an owl's cry bodes ill for those near by has been the main folk tradition concerning the bird in Europe.[1] John Ruskin could exclaim: 'Whatever wise people may say of them, I at least myself have found the owl's cry always prophetic of mischief to me' (Armstrong, p. 114). The Nightingale draws on all of these associations to condemn the Owl in the first quarter of the poem, and repeats them all many times throughout.

Nightingales are also best known as birds of darkness, as their name 'night singer' implies, but they escape ill fame on this account because of their migratory habits. Cuckoos and nightingales are the first birds to return in spring: 'On the third of April (old style) / Come in the cuckoo and the nightingale' (Swainson, p. 19). Because the nightingale's cry signals the arrival of the warm season, the bird itself is welcome, and when medieval authors are not influenced by the classical Philomel story, they describe its song as 'merry.'[2] This merriness and the association with spring are the nightingale's chief traits in folklore. The Nightingale tries very hard to make her welcomeness to men the decisive factor in their rivalry, and indeed we respond positively to her description of her activities in lines 433–62.

Folk tradition concerning these birds may dictate even their setting in the poem. When introduced, the Nightingale is perched on a flowering spray and thus linked to an obvious symbol of the warm season she ushers in. The poet's choice of an 'old stoc' for the Owl suggests that he knew of the practice of some owls of 'pressing against the stem (stock) of a tree with unruffled feathers, so as to assimilate [themselves] to the stump, and elude notice' (Swainson, p. 130). The folk name of the eagle owl is 'stock owl' because of this habit. Moreover folklore links owls and ivy. This association appears in the famous holly and ivy carol 'Holy berith beris, beris rede ynowgh,' in verses of such later writers as Drayton and Shirley, and in the folk name for the tawny owl, 'ivy owl' (Swainson, p. 124). Hässler and Robertson take pains to prove these dwellings suitable allegorically and spiritually, but it is quite possible that they are primarily traditional.[3]

The conflict as it emerges in the opening lines is expressed in terms of these folk traditions and unadorned by the literary and philosophical issues which appear later. Indeed the pairing off of nightingale against owl may itself be a folk tradition.[4] In a manner suitable to such an antipathy, the poem commences not like a serious intellectual debate, but like a quarrel between children of different national, religious, or racial backgrounds: one, enjoying temporary safety from attack, tells the other to go away and chants a litany of trite insults.

The second type of tradition which makes a significant contribution to the poem is literary. In literary contexts the owl is again often known as a bird of ill omen, but frequently has as counterbalance a reputation for great wisdom. This reputation originates in the owl's almost human facial structure, and in its association with Athene, goddess of wisdom (Armstrong, pp. 117-24). The poet joins these folk and literary traditions in an unusual way. His Owl warns men of impending disaster, not so much as agent of providential intervention, but through her own innate knowledge of the future which is her 'wisdom': 'For ich am witi, ful iwis, / An wod al þat to kumen is' (1189-90) - and she proceeds to list the types of disasters she has the natural power to foretell. However she also boasts:

An ȝet ich con muchel more:
Ich con inoh in bokes lore,
An eke ich can of þe goddspelle
More þan ich nule þe telle;
For ich at chirche come ilome
An muche leorni of wisdome.
Ich wat al of þe tacninge
An of oþer feole þinge.

(1207-14)

This claim is obviously questionable; it is an extension of tradition, but is probably meant to be recognized as unjustifiable.

The literary traditions concerning nightingales associate them with love. From heralding spring (natural fact) to celebrating it (lore) is an easy step; men project their own joy into the bird's song. From there to the celebration of love is but another. Latin, Provençal, and French lyrics abound in verses joining nightingales, warm weather, and love; and since many of the love-relationships mentioned are not marital, nightingales became associated with illicit love and with the sensual rather than the spiritual side of human love affairs.[5] The Nightingale freely admits her connection with love, but vehemently denies that she encourages illicit passion. In assessing her character we have to decide how to interpret the discrepancy between her protestations and her general reputation.[6]

The contributions to the poem of folk and literary bird lore are straightforward, and have caused no major interpretative snarls. With religious lore it is far otherwise, the rub being that the sacred traditions are contradictory, and reference to them is almost never direct and unequivocal. We are probably justified in believing Genesis i: 28 to be behind the birds' notion that they should be judged according to their usefulness to man, but most religious influence is more problematical than this. The Owl, for instance, does not call herself a monk, but this identification (or at least a special relationship to monks) is implied when she boasts:

Ich singe an eue a riȝte time,
& soþþe won hit is bedtime,
Þe þridde siþe ad middelniȝte,
& so ich mine song adiȝte.
Wone ich iso arise vorre
Oþer dairim oþer daisterre,
Ich do god mid mine þrote
& warni men to hore note.

(323–30)

There is a traditional basis for her claim: Eadmer of Canterbury and others liken monks to owls (*PL* 159, cols. 699–700), probably influenced by the imagery of Psalm ci: 7–8: *factus sum sicut nycticorax in domicilio*, etc. Viewed in context this allusion to owls is very positive (indeed the only favourable mention of them in the Bible), and lends itself to equations between owls and ascetic recluses. In *De Bestiis et Aliis Rebus*, which is found under Hugh of St Victor's name though not actually by him (*PL* 177, col. 30) the author glosses the psalter lines *Moraliter autem nycticorax non quemlibet justum innuit nobis, sed eum qui, inter homines degens, ab intuitu hominum se, in quantum potest, abscondit.*

Lucem refugit, quia humanæ laudis gloriam non attendit. 'Monk' would fit his gloss quite as well as 'just man.'

'Hugh' also remarks in the same paragraph *Mystice nycticorax Christum significat*, which brings us to the Owl's second religious claim. Christ was killed by those He sought to aid and hung upon a rood; the Owl, despite her uniformly helpful intentions, is killed by men and hung upon a 'rodde' (1646) – and both Christ and the Owl continue to aid man after death despite such scurvy treatment. The Owl verges on blasphemous parody when she insists:

Þah hit beo soþ, ich do heom god
An for heom ich chadde mi blod.
Ich do heom god mid mine deaþe ...

(1615–17, italics added)

If these insinuations of monk-like and Christ-like stature are meant to be taken seriously, then the Owl enjoys considerable moral superiority to the relatively frivolous Nightingale. On the other hand, there are equally well-known religious traditions equating owls with Jews and sinners. Owls are 'unclean' in most Biblical contexts, and hence the similitude to the spiritually unclean. They love darkness, which translates symbolically to loving the darkness of error or evil. The little birds who attack during daylight become then good Christians chastising the sinner in their midst. This motif of owl mobbed by little birds was a favourite with misericord carvers,[7] and the owl as Jew is the principal moral extracted from the owl in the *Bestiary*.[8] Since it is her enmity with little birds that lets the Owl operate both as Christly scarecrow and lure[9] (these, her two strongest claims to worth, appear in lines 1607–17 and 1625–30), and that enmity has unfavourable connotations, we might well feel that her Christly pretentions are being undercut. We might also wonder if this likeness to Jew or sinner attacked by the righteous is meant to influence our reception of earlier passages concerning her warfare with little birds. Should it colour our response near the end of the poem (1658–72) where a chorus of birds presses about the Owl threateningly, rejoicing at her supposed defeat?

Religious traditions concerning nightingales are equally mixed. The Nightingale makes a claim very like the Owl's to religious stature:

Clerkes, munekes & kanunes,
Þar boþ þos gode wicketunes,
Ariseþ up to midelniȝte
An singeþ of þe houene liȝte,
An prostes upe londe singeþ
Wane þe liȝt of daie springeþ.
An ich hom helpe wat i mai:
Ich singe mid hom niȝt & dai;
An ho boþ alle for me þe gladdere
An to þe songe boþ þe raddere.
Ich warni men to here gode
Þat hi bon bliþe on hore mode ...

(729–40)

No critic equates her with a monk and indeed there is no traditional sanction known to me for such an identification, but she does seem to be demanding recognition as a religious figure of some sort, and in terms almost identical with her enemy's. Possibly she looks on herself as a cheerful, love-oriented servant of God of the sort made popular by St Francis, or possibly she is just a 'chorister of divine love.' Alcuin (*PL* 101, cols. 803–4) writes of a nightingale in this exalted vein, as do much later writers like Bonaventura (?), John of Howden, and John Lydgate. Some critics, however, ignore her protestations entirely; to them, she remains a frivolous and immoral chatterer. In favour of this stand are various anecdotes about saints who found nightingale song far from conducive to devotion:

There is a story of Edward the Confessor which relates how, annoyed by the songs which interrupted his devotions, he prayed that nightingales might never be heard at Havering atte Bower in Essex ... There is also a saying that since a hermit cursed the nightingales at St Leonards they have never returned to the proscribed area. (Armstrong, pp. 187–8)

These saints are pre-Franciscan and doubtless of the Owl's gloomy persuasion, but their conviction of the nightingale's unhelpfulness is worth recording. And of course the Nightingale's reputed tie to carnal love goes far to weaken her demands for spiritual recognition. She is, in fact, quite as seriously undercut as the Owl.

The most troublesome aspect of this religious lore is determining whether it is relevant or not. Aside from the birds' claims to religious worth and their views on how man best prepares his soul for heaven, no sacred traditions are explicitly mentioned in the text. The Owl does not say 'I am a monk'; she merely boasts of singing at specified intervals during the night, a practice which resembles a monk's singing night offices, but which may be interpreted in purely avian terms. So too may the scarecrow-crucifixion, which reflects actual farm practice. There are many colourful pieces of religious lore pertaining to these birds; some like the Jew/sinner simile widely known, others nonce-formations.[10] The author probably knew many such similes and may have intended the audience's knowledge of them to influence its response, but at this remove in time and culture we cannot determine which are relevant and which not. Future students of the poem should note that it is unwise to build an interpretation which depends for validity on the presence of any one piece of religious lore; not only can such traditions not be proven relevant, but the critic cannot insure his reading against being undercut by contradictory lore whose very presence may be unknown to him. If the author meant the poem to be read in terms of a few specific traditions, then we shall never be able to interpret it with certainty. On the other hand, the plurality of possibilities may be intentional, the ambiguities deliberate. A reading consonant with this state of affairs is altogether a more hopeful enterprise.

When we consider the use critics have made of the various types of traditions, we find that until recently few used them at all. Hinckley, Atkins, and Huganir traced and analysed various pieces of lore, but looked on them more as sources than as interpretative tools. Robertson and Hässler drew on a few specific traditions to support their arguments, but failed to consider other, often contradictory, possibilities. But with Iser, Donovan, and Peterson (particularly the last two), we find systematic attempts to utilize the traditions for interpreting the whole poem.

Iser does not bother to analyse the traditions carefully, and offers merely a hasty differentiation between Owl (gloom and ill omen) and the Nightingale (spring-herald, celebrator of love, and singer of divine praise); but he does make a very interesting point (p. 315):

> Die Nachtigall glaubt, die Eule durch traditionelle Anschauungen entscheidend treffen zu können. Die Eule hingegen entwickelt aus den Anwürfen der Nachtigall Aspekte, die nicht zur Tradition des *topos* gehören, deren Evidenz aber die Nachtigall überrascht und für Augenblicke entwaffnet.

The Nightingale's anxiety is noted in lines 391 ff., 659 ff., 933 ff., and 1291 ff. The unconventional elements in the Owl's defence include her claims to noble (i.e. hawkish) precedent for her weapons and enmity with little birds, her defence of the aesthetics of her song, and her reasons for preferring winter. In her attacks on the Nightingale, she deviates from tradition in accusing the Nightingale of living near privies and of eating spiders, flies, and grubs, and in her insistence that the Nightingale's only virtue – her song – is worthless, even unpleasant to man.[11] Iser's remarks are only incidental to his main concern, the blending of literary forms in this work, but he does touch on an important difference in use of traditions. He helps explain why the Nightingale is apparently so flustered at times, something no one else had done satisfactorily.

Mortimer J. Donovan's article is an attempt to interpret *The Owl and the Nightingale* entirely on the basis of the scriptural commentaries on Deuteronomy xiv: 12–16, Leviticus xi: 16, and Psalm ci: 7–8. The *noctua* and *bubo* of the first two are unclean, and usually glossed as sinners who flee the light; the *nycticorax* of the psalm signifies Christ or 'the just man.' Donovan argues that the Nightingale mistakes the Owl for a *noctua* and accuses her of all the *noctua*'s vices, whereas she is actually a *nycticorax*, the benevolent altruist, even as the Nightingale is a chorister of divine love, not an inciter to lust as the Owl avers. This interpretation, though excitingly neat, does not explain (to my satisfaction, at least) some of the issues contested, such as astrology. Nor does it justify the assertion that both birds are 'really' only what their favourable traditions make them. On what grounds can the bad traditions be dismissed? Further, Donovan treats the birds as serious religious figures but does not attempt to explain away their gross lapses from logic and disreputable desire to win at all costs. Finally, he makes no attempt to explain why the poem exists: are all eighteen hundred lines just an elaborate scriptural word play, an overblown pun? Donovan's essay is clearly important because of his effort to face squarely the contradictory nature of the traditions (even within the limited group deriving from the Bible), but the reading he gives seems distorted because of his one-sided valuation of the contestants and because of his exclusive concentration upon the serious and religious side of the poem.

Douglas L. Peterson views *The Owl and the Nightingale* as a debate between a logician (representing Christian wisdom) and a rhetorician (arguing for sensuality). His fundamental assumption is that all the Owl's righteous self praise and denigrating accusations are true, and that all the Nightingale says is false. For example, he dismisses as preposterous the Nightingale's assertion that she too helps people towards heaven; yet Alcuin and Bonaventura found nothing unworthy in that idea. Peterson ignores the fact that both birds are associated with both good and bad traditions. Indeed, their claims and charges are extraordinarily similar, and any critic who thinks one is to be preferred *must* show why the traditions he wants to ignore or depreciate are irrelevant.

The range and variation among the traditions concerning these birds is vast, and because of the manner in which the lore is used, not limitable. The scholars who have uncovered beliefs and associations lost in the intervening centuries have definitely added to our comprehension and enjoyment of the poem, but we are not able to pronounce which traditions are unequivocally relevant. The Jew/sinner simile relating to the Owl for instance was *very* widely known, yet there is no clear textual evidence that the author had it in mind in any of the passages mentioning the Owl's enmity with day birds. Its applicability would sour and discredit the Owl's highest claims; proof of its irrelevance would make the Owl appear very grand – at least at times. We simply cannot demonstrate the presence or absence of lore not explicitly mentioned, and very few religious traditions are alluded to directly. Hence, we have to recognize that interpretations based on selected traditions can only be offered as unsupportable hypotheses, and anyone who claims validity is not justified in doing so.

Any chance of firm interpretation lies in accepting such ambiguity as both intentional and significant. I would argue that the precise interpretation of any one point is meant to be vague, that the possibilities are deliberately contradictory. Because this is a quarrel over worth, each bird makes great claims for herself, but the author sees to it that most such boasts can be undercut by conflicting traditions. This constant movement to diminish the speakers through ridicule, as I shall argue later, is a common satiric technique. The birds, precisely because they are the inheritors of conflicting traditions, are natural vehicles for satire. As Owst remarks concerning the use of animal symbolism in preaching (pp. 240–1):

> '"*Factus sum sicut nicticorax in domicilio*" that is to sey – "I am made as a niʒtraven in the evesynges of a howse"'. Who, then, was indicated by the bird in question? – obviously, 'thes peple of religion', continually 'preyng on nightes', that 'dwellen in houses ioyned to the chirch', 'as munkes, chanones, nunnes, ankers, and hankeresses'. To be called a night-raven of this kind was distinctly a compliment. But what, indeed – when another species of 'night-bird' is chosen as a figure of those that love the darkness rather than the light, because their deeds are evil! [i.e. *bubo* or *noctua*] *Here we get material for the production of a satire* (final italics added).

Keeping the possibility of satiric interpretation in mind, I would like to turn now to the second avian problem, the reasons for the author's employing animal protagonists.

Little has been written on the relationship between *The Owl and the Nightingale* and other poems with animal principals. The beast fables have been sifted for similarities and motifs because they obviously were known to the author: two are retold as exempla in the course of the debate, and others seem to be alluded to. Furthermore, fable collections were extremely popular from the last quarter of the twelfth century on into the thirteenth.[12] The beast epic, however, has been ignored, as have the English and French bird debates and parliaments. Yet most of the epics and the earliest parliament poems date from before 1200, although the most famous are admittedly later.[13] Since no source for *The Owl and the Nightingale* is known, we should at least examine these related works for similarities and differences. We cannot look for the sorts of likenesses normally found in sources, but even from late works we can pick up ideas on the possible functions of animal protagonists by asking ourselves what these authors gained by using animals. Why did some choose birds? What is the essential nature of these other works? What seems to be their *raison d'être*? Are they, for instance, plot-, character-, or idea-oriented?[14]

Examination of the fables, beast epics, English bird debates, French bird parliaments, and Chaucer's *Parliament of Fowls* indicates a variety of advantages gained by the authors using animal protagonists. One advantage evident in the fables is a depersonalizing and generalizing of the principals in order to make the moral more universal. A lion as king is preferable to King Louis IX if the author does not want our feelings about the specific monarch to cloud the basic issues of his fable. Animals may add incidental humour, and animals with pronounced traits (the fox for cunning) may exemplify with particular felicity the moral types they represent, but the basic function of the animals is to generalize.

In the beast epic, generalization is less important than depersonalization and dehumanization. When the vassal of a human king kills or maims his fellows, we do not laugh, and the villain can only be feared and hated. If, however, the king is a bumbling lion, the murderous vassal a fox, and his victims the chickens, the bear, and the cat, we do not feel so involved. Our whole perspective is changed by animals standing in for humans and as a result we see the fox as a trickster-hero, not an archvillain. We look forward to seeing how he will get out of each scrape, and tend to feel pleased when he succeeds. The use of animals here clearly provides a comic distancing which frees the plot of all immediate seriousness, simply because we cannot really believe in the animals. They talk importantly about feudal law procedures and supposedly live in castles, but obviously they *really* live in a world where raiding a priest's hen run is a major undertaking. Consequently, we are not inclined to take any portion of their adventures very seriously, even the pain Renard's victims suffer. The comic distancing of serious issues is the most notable advantage conferred by animals in the beast epics, but it should be noted that secondarily they offer opportunities for satire on and parody of human institutions.[15]

The avian principals in the bird debates and parliament poems all serve to distance the reader from the subject, but less markedly for comedy than for letting the author present material that would be immoral, frivolous, or implausible with human actors. Courtly love, for instance, which places unchristian value on passionate interpersonal relationships, and subordinates male to female, would in many contexts be the object of moral indignation or derision. In stylish St Valentine's day poems however concepts of love can be bandied about playfully, and the preposterous upheld: thus in *The Cuckoo and the Nightingale*, the lovesick swain (nightingale) is allowed to triumph over the sturdy cynic (cuckoo). In clerk and knight debates, clerks are declared superior to knights as lovers, an immoral conclusion to a frivolous question. Moreover, had the plot been enacted by humans, it would have fallen to pieces, for what knight would serve as champion for clerks on this issue in a trial by combat?

Parliament of Fowls would likewise be implausible with human actors, for men do not take wives at a seasonal mating; neither do they gather for some other reason yet fall to discussing and acting out love-dilemmas. Of course this freedom from plausible realism can be abused. *The Thrush and the Nightingale* is a feeble poem, but its weaknesses would be even more glaring with human actors: what man would assert *in earnest* 'Among a þousent leuedies i-tolde / Þer nis non wickede I holde' (52–3)? A more sensible poet, wishing to make intelligent remarks on female status, would have shown the nightingale ready to concede some of women's faults while still holding out the example of the Virgin to defeat the thrush's total denigration of the sex. Even Dunbar, who was capable of better, lets the colourful avian surface substitute for genuine thought in his *The Merle and the Nychtingaill*, where the two debate on carnal love and love of God, the religious nightingale effecting an unmotivated *volte-face* in the lusty merle.

If we inquire why these authors chose to use birds, we do not find clear-cut answers. One reason would seem to be that such choice was conventional: birds were inevitable denizens of the courtly love garden landscape, and authors with love-question 'plots' evidently felt that birds were suitable actors. From mere background details, the birds became songsters with a definite role (*La Messe des Oiseaux*), then vassals of Cupid (the clerk-knight debates) and of Venus (*De Venus la Deesse d'Amor*). In these capacities, they give instruction and sermons on true love, debate love questions, fight combats, and handle the daily business of the courtly love world. Since the author of *The Owl and the Nightingale* discusses love, adultery, and sins of the flesh, his decision to use birds may have been influenced by the new but growing convention that birds could deal with such subjects.[16]

A more important advantage offered by the use of birds is the particular lore associated with each species which can be used to reinforce the human traits being considered under animal guise. Bird lore func-

tions thus in *The Cuckoo and the Nightingale* and *Parliament of Fowls.*
In the former, the cuckoo's cynical view of romantic love is appropriate
to its lore reputation, which derives from the sound of its name (evoca-
tive of cuckold) and from its habit of laying its eggs in other birds' nests.
In *Parliament of Fowls*, the traditional valuation of the birds is used to
suggest and reinforce their roles as members of different classes of society. The falcons are noble in medieval lore, associated with the noble
pursuit of hunting, and hence fit easily the role of high-born lovers.
Ducks and geese could not have been used for those parts because of
their barnyard associations, but fit well as the gabbling, plebeian mob.
As we have already seen, bird lore suggests human characteristics for the
protagonists in *The Owl and the Nightingale*, and it is probably for their
equivalently contradictory traditions that these particular birds were
chosen.

If we try to describe the nature of these different sorts of animal-
centred works, we find that most can be characterized as idea-oriented.
That is, they exist to express an intellectual concept (like *Pearl*) rather
than to present an entertaining intrigue (as does the *Miller's Tale*) or
character study (*Troilus*). The beast epic, to be sure, is often plot-
oriented; our interest centres on what is going to happen next. But
in all the others, one could hardly say there is a plot at all. The fable's
reason for existing is to communicate its most famous feature, the moral.
French parliament poems are concerned with the idea of whether a knight
or clerk makes the better lover. And in the other English bird debates,
one's chief reaction is likely to be regret that the 'idea' is not more substantial, for plot and character are so utterly lacking that the idea – such
as it is – is all.

The concept of idea-orientation, though it helps us describe the basic
thrust of these works, is not fully satisfactory. The triviality of many of
the ideas makes us think that something more important to the authors
must have made them go to the trouble of writing. The author of *The
Thrush and the Nightingale* may have composed that poem as a defence of women against the usual satiric detractions, but if so, he
failed to do a convincing job. It seems more likely, when we consider
the ending, that he really designed the poem as a tribute to the Virgin,
in which case his real purpose, devotion, is extrinsic to the superficial
concerns of the poem itself. Another possibility which excludes neither
expression of an idea nor devotion is that the poet is showing off his skill

at versification. *The Merle and the Nychtingaill* definitely exhibits both showpiece and devotional qualities, and so does *The Cuckoo and the Nightingale*, though the devotion in the latter is parodic, offered to the 'God of Love.' The stylized French parliament poems, lacking the inner tension of an important idea, may also be primarily showpieces. And the *Parliament of Fowls*, though it has a good deal more intellectual substance than these others, also seems to be something of a display piece.[17]

To sum up what we can deduce from other beast-centred works: we see that the use of animals (1) generalizes the actors so as to make moral lessons universally applicable; (2) may create a comic distancing which lets the author raise serious issues without preaching and without upsetting his listeners; and (3) frees the author from the demands of probability, letting him present a plot or idea which would be awkward or impossible with human actors. The actual choice of birds rather than beasts in *The Owl and the Nightingale* seems best explained by the specific folk, literary, and religious traits which these particular birds can bring to the conflict, and possibly by the French convention that birds have a special connection with love and the intellectual issues associated with love. And finally, a glance at these other works strongly suggests that desire to display the author's skills may be partly responsible for the composition of the poem, especially since no one idea emerges in the birds' arguments which might constitute the poem's reason for existing. Some critics who believe Nicholas of Guildford to be the poet have indeed argued that the poem's principal aim is to display his talents. Though this explanation does not fully satisfy my desire to know what the poem 'means,' and I do not think it the whole answer, I agree that such an extrinsic aim is consonant with some of the poem's puzzling features.

I have theorized long enough about the functions of non-human protagonists. Let us turn to the poem and see whether such abstractions help us understand the way the poem works. Try to imagine, for instance, what the piece would be like if two village women – a sombre widow and a gaily dressed young housewife – were to take the birds' places. There would be scope for some brilliantly funny exchanges – perhaps in the manner of Dunbar's flytings – but some issues would become much more serious. By the time the wife had passed the point of reviling the widow for foretelling and enjoying others' misfortunes, and had begun to insinuate that the widow *caused* the troubles through witchcraft (corresponding to the remarks of lines 1233–50, 1298–1316), the argument would be getting out of hand. The human consequences of a witchcraft charge are too serious for us to take them lightly; a person so charged might very well be killed. Likewise anyone proven to encourage and aid adultery could be punished for treason towards the wronged husband (if he were of high rank) and would go to hell in any case.

Changing the nature of the protagonists greatly alters the poem's impact. With humans, the author would have to cast the work as a complete farce (doing away with any serious import) or as a very serious indictment of human follies, for either the meaning of the harsher accusations would have to be so distanced that we did not fully respond, or else we would be forced to recognize the debate for what it would be – a bitterly nasty quarrel displaying all that is vicious and unworthy in mankind. And our listening would merit Virgil's rebuke in *Inferno* XXX, line 148: *chè voler ciò udire è bassa voglia.* The use of birds allows the poet to work a compromise between the farcical and the serious. Issues such as witchcraft; enticement to sin; and being repellent when alive, welcome only when dead, can be brought up here with all the venom the contestants would naturally express. We may contemplate the charges in earnest when thinking the poem over afterwards, but we do not need to feel greatly sorry for the birds when the accusations are made because we do not altogether believe in the reality of the birds' emotions.

In trying to understand the effect that using birds has, we should consider one point more – to what extent are these figures birds and to what extent men? How is their dual nature joined? And how do different methods of joining human and animal change the impact?

If we see a cat smoking a cigar in a cartoon, the incongruous sight is amusing, but implies no moral valuation of either cat or cigar-smoking, for the cat is wholly animal, and smoking an act morally neutral. If an animal unwittingly performs an act considered wrong in a human context, and if this act is pointed out for men to see, the act can serve as an indictment of mankind, since an animal cannot sin: the fathers of the church were wont to draw morals from animal lust, or from such material as a dog's returning to his own vomit, which to them signified the inveterate sinner returning to his sin. Or a purely human sin can be grafted onto an animal; this combination is clearly meant to criticize man – the Owl's boasting of her booklearning is of this sort. Finally, an animal may perform an act which is animal, but interpretable as human: the Nightingale's singing in spring is natural, yet under the influence of literary lore may be construed as incitement to lust and celebration of sensual love. This type of combination leads us into a hall of mirrors – we cannot tell whether an act is a reflection of animal practice or reflects a human endeavour disguised as animal practice. This type of combination characterizes the bulk of the poem: we are unable to say with certainty whether the Owl's singing at night is just her natural habit or an important clue to her religious stature. Throughout the poem, the birds seem to remain birds, but show enough human traits to make explication of any one act exceedingly difficult.

This confusing interplay between avian and human, between the neutral and the morally charged, should remind us of the similar ambiguities concerning good and bad traditions discussed at the beginning of this chapter. The avian nature of the protagonists is responsible for all these complex dualities. It provides the material for the continuous movement of setting up and knocking down, for the building and undercutting, contrasting and contradicting. Such dualities and incongruities are the natural milieu of satire – and their presence and function in the poem are perhaps the most important aspect of the protagonists' avian nature.

NOTES

1 For information on the lore pertaining to the birds, see Rev Charles Swainson's *Provincial Names and Folk Lore of British Birds*, English Dialect Society (London: Trübner 1885), also published with altered title as Publications of the Folk-Lore Society 17 (London: Elliot Stock 1886); and Edward A. Armstrong's *The Folklore of Birds* (London: Collins 1958).

2 *Proverbs, Sentences, and Proverbial Phrases From English Writings Mainly Before 1500* (Cambridge, Mass.: Harvard University Press 1968) by Bartlett. Jere Whiting with the collaboration of Helen Wescott Whiting gives an entry (N 110) to the merriness of the nightingale.

3 Herbert Hässler, *'The Owl and the Nightingale' und die literarischen Bestrebungen des 12. und 13. Jahrhunderts* (Frankfurt 1942?) 94–7; and D.W. Robertson, Jr, 'Historical Criticism' 24–5

4 Hinckley (*PMLA* [1929] 343–5) collected evidence of such a traditional pairing, though none of it is English. I suspect that the two are linked in proverb and this poem not because of some specific tradition of enmity, but because their lore traits are naturally opposing qualities. This sort of reason lies behind their joint appearance in *Le Roman de la Rose*, 5943–7.

5 See Thomas Alan Shippey, 'Listening to The Nightingale' *Comparative Literature* 22 (1970) 46–60.

6 A number of details in the poem may stem from minor literary traditions. The author may well have learned from the writings of Giraldus Cambrensis or

Alexander Neckam that nightingales do not sing in various northern lands (see Atkins, p. lxviii and Huganir, p. 99). The story of the punishing of a nightingale may reflect knowledge of Marie de France's *Laustic* or Neckam's *De Naturis Rerum*. The charge of dirtiness laid to the Owl may stem from written fables; indeed the author uses a form of the falcon's nest fable for illustrating that charge. But that accusation may be derived as plausibly either from folklore or from the biblical notion of 'unclean.' For evidence on these alternatives, see Hinckley's 'Science and Folk-lore in *The Owl and the Nightingale*' *PMLA* 47 (1932) 303–14, Donovan, p. 213, and Atkins, p. lxviii.

7 See Faith Medlin's *Centuries of Owls in Art and the Written Word* (Norwalk, Conn.: Silvermine Publishers 1967) 34. She lists English churches preserving carvings of this motif as Norwich, Beverly Minster, Bishop's Stortford, Ludlow, Ely, and Wells.

8 See Florence McCulloch's *Mediaeval Latin and French Bestiaries*, University of North Carolina Studies in the Romance Languages and Literatures 33 (Chapel Hill, N.C.: University of North Carolina Press 1960) 147–8.

9 The owl used as lure appears in a marginal picture in MS Arundel 83, f.14. Judging from its blank eyes, it is dead, possibly stuffed. See Lilian M.C. Randall, *Images in the Margins of Gothic Manuscripts* (Berkeley and Los Angeles: University of California Press 1966) figure 338.

10 Examples of such miscellaneous (and probably extraneous) traditions include Walter Map's likening creatures of the night such as *noctua*, *nycticorax*, and *bubo* to corrupt judicial officials who fatten their purses at the expense of those they are supposed to be helping (*De Nugis Curialium* I, x). Thomas of Cantempré in his *De Naturis Rerum* (lib. V, art. 18) compares the owl to dissolute clerics who take fat benefices and defile the church; Hugh of St Cher (Venice 1732 edition I, iii^v) sees the owl fighting little birds as equivalent to Herod's beheading John the Baptist. I am indebted to Robert E. Kaske for these last two significations. Neither one is generally known.

11 Iser does not seem to have been aware that the Owl is not alone in finding the Nightingale's incessance objectionable. Armstrong (p. 187) states:

> the nightingale's song has not always rendered it beloved ... A poet of the Greek anthology protested,
>
> *Leaf-loving nightingales, loquacious sex,*
> *Sleep quietly, I beg, and cease your din.*
>
> More recently, Girton girls have complained that the nightingales interfered with their studies ...

Nor have other critics recognized the possible justice of the Owl's complaint. Hinckley (*PMLA* [1932] 309–10) says 'When the Owl calls the Nightingale a chatterbox, she voices a sentiment characteristic of the Philistine, who, in every age, has resented what is beautiful. It is like Dr Johnson's calling *Lycidas* "disgusting."' But Hinckley admits in a puzzled way that there are references to nightingales in a similar vein in classical literature.

12 Several medieval collections in prose and verse, Latin, French, and English, could have been known to the author of this poem even if he wrote before 1216. Among those most likely to have been available in England were the *Romulus Neveletii* of Walter the Englishman (*ca.* 1175), the pseudo-Alfredian collection (probably Middle English) now lost but known to Marie de France, Marie's own collection (*ca.* 1170), Alexander Neckam's *Novus Aesopus* (1217), and the York Fragment (*ca.* 1200). For information on the author's use of fables, see Hinckley, *PMLA* (1929) 347–52, Huganir, pp. 15–50, and Atkins, pp. lxiii–lxvii, 196–200.

13 The accepted dates for branches I–XII, XIV, and XVII of *Le Roman de Renard* are 1174–1205, and the Latin *Ysengrimus* is even earlier (*ca.* 1150). Among the French parliaments, the Anglo-Norman *Melior et Ydoine* and all five manuscripts of *Le Jugement D'Amours* date from the turn of the thirteenth century. (Charles Oulmont has edited these in *Les Débats du Clerc et du Chevalier* [Paris: Librairie Honoré Champion 1911].) *De Venus la Deesse d'Amor* has been edited by Wendelin Foerster (Bonn: Max Cohen & Sohn 1880) and *La Messe des Oiseaux* of Jean de Condé has been edited by Jacques Ribard (Genève: Librairie Droz 1970). The English bird debate closest to our poem in date is *The Thrush and the Nightingale* (*ca.* 1250–1300), edited by Bruce Dickins and R.M. Wilson in *Early Middle English Texts* (Cambridge, England: Bowes and Bowes 1951) 71–6. *The Cuckoo and the Nightingale* (*ca.* 1400), otherwise known as *The Boke of Cupide*, has been edited by Erich Vollmer (Berlin: E. Ebering 1898), and *The Merle and the Nychtingaill* (*ca.* 1500) in *The Poems of William Dunbar* (1932; reprint, London: Faber and Faber 1960) edited by W. Mackay Mackenzie, pp. 134–7.

14 R.S. Crane makes this distinction in his essay 'The Concept of Plot and the Plot of *Tom Jones*' in *Critics and Criticism* (Chicago: University of Chicago Press 1952) 616–47, especially p. 620.

15 The effect of comic distancing and parody is also felt in the French parliament poems. See, for instance, the bird combat in *Le Jugement D'Amours*. There, the two champions (the nightingale and the popinjay), donning flower-coloured armour and exchanging ceremonious challenges are amusing; in Shakespeare's *Richard II*, the identical actions are anything but funny.

16 The chances of the author having heard one of these clerk-knight debates are fairly good. Not only do some seem to date back to 1200 or earlier, but some were Anglo-Norman, and one was apparently written in English. The poet of *Le Geste de Blancheflour e de Florence* (Oulmont, p. 183) states:

> Banastre en englois le fist,
> E Brykhulle cest escrit
> En franceois translata.

(427–9)

17 *Parliament of Fowls*, the most famous of the bird parliament poems, offers a unique parallel to *The Owl and the Nightingale*. Like the latter, it is not plot- or character-oriented; nor is it precisely devotional. Though the idea-content is very prominent, the issue is not clear-cut as in other parliament poems or

debates, and aside from agreement that love is the theme, there is no consensus on what is being said about love or what the poem means. Critics have tried to read the work as a political or social allegory, as an intellectual or philosophical treatise, and have worried about its form and possible sources with so little luck that there is no accord on such basic issues as whether the male falcons are meant to seem silly or admirable.

the significance of the debate form

Examination of the avian protagonists is one method of approaching the poem; study of the literary form is another. *The Owl and the Nightingale* is a debate or altercation, and we can learn a great deal about the piece by comparing it with other examples of the genre. Regrettably, little study of this sort has been undertaken because Wells concluded discouragingly that 'very often the "similarities" [to other debates] are really not such at all' (p. lxii). Because Wells can be believed when he says he has made a 'careful study and comparison of practically all the extant contention poems earlier than the fourteenth century in the three languages [Provençal, Latin, and French]' (p. lvi), subsequent scholars have assumed that Wells exhausted the subject. This is not the case: although Wells's study will probably remain definitive for the parallels he analysed, others need to be explored. In this chapter, I shall attempt to throw further light on *The Owl and the Nightingale*, first by analysing relevant portions of the debate tradition and relating the discoveries to the poem; next by examining the poem's puzzling ending, for the resolution is naturally the focal feature of any debate; and last by assessing the readings built upon considerations of form or ending. As in the foregoing chapter, my conclusions will be as much cautionary and theoretical as constructive; nonetheless, I hope to be able to demonstrate that we can derive quite a number of precise expectations regarding the most probable methods of interpreting the poem.

Although the medieval debate poem clearly descends from such classical forms as the contention eclogue (Virgil's third) and the general combat (Prudentius' *Psychomachia*), the oldest *altercationes* date from Carolingian times.[1] Among these earliest pieces however are found most of the features which characterize the form throughout subsequent development: Theodulus' *Eclogue* has human debaters, the rest have non-human – Alcuin(?)'s *Conflictus* is fought by the seasons winter and spring, Ermoldus Nigellus' *Carmen* is a contest between two rivers, and Sedulius Scotus' *Certamen* describes the strife between a rose and a lily.[2] All four have judge figures. In some one party wins, in others the debaters are reconciled. The subjects debated include both intellectual issues like religion, and personalia such as which contestant is most pleasing, welcome, and useful to man.

Once the debate form has left the Carolingian schoolroom and entered the vernacular, the poems are usually classified as *tenson, jeu-parti* or *partimen*, and feigned *tenson*. Wells used these terms to categorize those of the poem's features which are paralleled in continental works: debate arising from personalities, abusive language (*tenson*), verdict not given though a judge named, use of proverbs (*jeu-parti*), and narrative frame and the burst of song to honour the victor (feigned *tenson*). But since he admits that the author of *The Owl and the Nightingale* could have arrived at these features without reference to the European works, he concludes that inquiry into the debate tradition does not yield much of significance to studies of the poem. I suggest that it will be more profitable to cut across lingual and terminological boundaries and classify the poems according to whether they have human or non-human contestants, and see what characteristics emerge from these new groupings.

A list of the better known debates with human principals includes such works as *Altercatio Phyllidis et Florae* (along with its French imitations *Florence et Blancheflor, Hueline et Aiglantine*, and *Melior et Ydoine* – all clerk-knight debates), *Marguet Convertie, De Ganymede et Helena, Discussio litis super hereditate Lazari*, Theodulus' *Eclogue, Altercatio Rusticorum et Clericorum, De Presbytero et Logico, De Mauro et Zoilo, De Clarevallensibus et Cluniacensibus*, and *Quondam fuit factus festus*.[3] If we look at the issues at stake, we find abstract discussions of love quite common: the clerk-knight debates natter over which would be preferable as lover; *Marguet Convertie* traces in sing-song verse the whore's repentance as a result of a virtuous man's arguments; *De Ganymede et Helena* assesses homosexual and heterosexual love without offering either a convincing defence. The *Discussio litis super hereditate Lazari* is rather unusual, in that the subject could genuinely be debated in real life were the circumstances to arise – Lazarus, returning from the dead, wishes to reclaim his property, his sister insisting that it is legally hers. Though deriving from a religious story, this debate is really legal; the rest mentioned are all essentially religious. Pseustis and Alithia in Theodulus' *Eclogue*, both erudite sheeptenders, clash over religious doctrine, Alithia being Christian, Pseustis pagan. Variance in religious practices is the subject of *De Mauro et Zoilo, De Clarevallensibus et Cluniacensibus*, and *Quondam fuit factus festus. Altercatio Rusticorum et Clericorum* concerns lay versus ecclesiastical; *De Presbytero et Logico* is an argument over the proper use of learning. All of these subjects could be described roughly as intellectual; they are concerned with abstractions and theory, with variations in codified practices, with philosophies of living. Though the quality of thought involved in most is abysmal, it is in the intellectual arena that these poems are meant to compete.

Poems employing non-human protagonists include the debates between seasons,[4] Chardry's *Le Petit Plet*, whose principals are Youth and Age, Sedulius' *Certamen*, the anonymous *The Violet and the Rose, Conflictus Ovis et Lini*, Ermoldus Nigellus' *Carmen*, and various wine and water disputes.[5] In all of these, the fundamental conflict stems from natural, innate differences which the opponents could not change if they wished. Moreover, among contestants of the same natural order or function – bird, flower, river and fibre producer – it seems to be conventional to argue in terms of usefulness to man. Thus the two rivers quarrel fiercely over which does more in man's service; the flower pairs, like Nightingale and Owl, draw on religious and literary lore to support their claims to supremacy,[6] while the sheep and flax plant cite the Bible as authority for their claims, much as the birds use the proverbs of Alfred. Indeed, these last two contestants, like the birds, end by associating themselves with Christ, and both readily descend to 'shitwords.' In wine and water disputes we frequently find the same sort of squabble for man's favour, the use of authorities, and the unlaundered language, all features which seem to be typical of the altercations which grow out of the natural, lore-oriented differences found among non-human contestants.

Alas for neatness's sake, there is one group of debates which defy my handy general distinction: *The Cuckoo and the Nightingale, The Thrush and the Nightingale*, and *The Merle and the Nychtingaill* all argue over abstract intellectual issues despite their non-human principals. However, in trying to place *The Owl and the Nightingale* within the spectrum of debate issue orientation, we must recognize that non-human contestants may be related to intellectual issues in various ways. Two geese arguing over the nature of Christ are just mouthpieces for a purely human concern. The principals of these other English bird debates are like such geese. A different sort of poem emerges if two birds argue over nest building, even if they refer to man's architecture and the biblical specifications of Noah's ark. Such birds have a much closer relationship to their words. *The Owl and the Nightingale* resembles its fellow English poems far less than it does *Conflictus Ovis et Lini, Rosae Liliique Certamen*, and some of the wine-water debates. In all of these latter the quarrel arises from natural differences, though it sometimes extends to practices (and hence can be called 'intellectual' at times). In all, the arguments may be supported with allusions to human wisdom, proverbial or written, and may on occasion stray to strictly human issues – the Nightingale and Owl bicker over adultery. But if such intellectual issues enter, it is helter-skelter *via* the natural traits and lore, not as clearly defined, intellectual propositions to be argued over in scholastic fashion, as is the case in *The Thrush and the Nightingale*. And if human issues are to be discussed by non-humans, the convention seems to be quite firm that such issues be clearly set out, not disguised or half-transposed into non-human terms.

This distinction is extremely important to criticism of *The Owl and the Nightingale*. Atkins, Owst, Colgrave, and Robertson all formulate propositions which they believe to be the poem's theme. But in other debates with non-human protagonists we find no such intellectual concerns except usefulness to man. If *The Owl and the Nightingale* really is a treatise on types of poetry or on sensuality, with these human concerns being presented in avian disguise, it is departing radically from the pattern of its nearest formal analogues and anyone suggesting such an interpretation must take special pains to support it.

Since any quarrel becomes a fight for supremacy, the outcome of a debate is its natural focus. Everything builds towards the resolution; the meaning of the whole fight, and consequently of the debate form, is determined by the conclusion. Because the ending can be so important

to understanding an altercation, it seems logical to examine *The Owl
and the Nightingale*'s finale in this generic context, for the poem's ending is certainly problematical and might be crucial.

At the height of the argument, the Nightingale suddenly claims victory on the basis of a legal technicality, a supposed blunder in the Owl's
pleading. Few critics have actually paid attention to the end of the birds'
debate, preferring to talk of the triumph of one or the other in general
terms, but anyone supporting an interpretation other than victory for
the Nightingale *must* explain how her claim can be set aside. The other
debates, both human and non-human, furnish us with a wide variety of
possible endings, and an analysis and classification of these endings can
help us interpret this troublesome feature of *The Owl and the Nightingale*.

A completed debate may end only two ways: one or the other contestant wins, or they draw. The following resolutions are found in the
poems previously discussed. In the conflict between the warm seasons
and winter, either the parties are reconciled (*Altercatio Yemis et Estatis*)
or winter is vanquished (Alcuin's *Conflictus* and a later *Conflictus*). Wine
wins in *Denudata Veritate* and *Goliae Dialogus*; in the *Desputoison du
Vin et de l'Iaue*, various kinds of wines (in a general combat rather than
debate) squabble for precedence, with the result that they are duly
ranked, but water is given a seat of honour above all; and in the three
Italian versions, water is actually victorious. In Theodulus' *Eclogue*, Alithia, supporter of Christianity, defeats the pagan Pseustis, even as in similarly religious works the Church always defeats the Synagogue or the
Christian the Jew and the *croisé* the *décroisé*.[7] Helen defeats Ganymede.
In the clerk and knight debates, the clerk-loving women and their nightingale champions are adjudged victorious in all but *Le Geste de Blancheflour
e de Florence*, in which Florence, lover of knights, and the popinjay win.
In the quarrel between clerks and rustics, the clerks win. In *De Presbytero et Logico*, the priest wins. The prior is defeated in *Quondam fuit
factus festus*. In *Petit Plet*, Youth has the last word. And in the English
bird debates, the nightingales are always victorious.

Analysing such results, we observe that the most pleasant, most attractive contestant wins *unless* one has an overwhelming moral superiority to
which the author feels obliged to bow. Thus Alithia, St Église, the Church,
the Christian, and other such religious figures *must* win, no matter how
pleasant or accomplished the opponent. Debates with less serious issues

at stake favour the more attractive contestant. Helen wins – she has some moral claim as well; so do wine, the abbot who allows his monks wine, the nightingale wherever she appears, and, in most instances, the clerk (who naturally seemed the more winsome to clerkly writers). Only if the author is a moralist do the less licentious or more austere of these trivial debaters win – water, for instance, over wine. On the basis of this evidence we could expect *The Owl and the Nightingale* to end either with a reconciliation (a common solution when the contestants are of the same biological order) or with the Nightingale winning unless the author attributed great moral superiority to the Owl, or were heavy handedly moralistic, something even the 'historical' critics of the poem agree he is not.

A light-hearted poet may let the more attractive contestant win. However, victory is no proof of the victor's fundamental superiority. If the relative immorality of clerk and knight as lovers can be weighed, then clerks are not likely to be the morally proper victors. And wine, though 'good for the stomach' and hallowed in certain religious respects, has not the virtuous austerity of water. Hence the earnest authors of some versions of these two debate families, preferring didacticism to humorous irony, ended the altercations with moralistic resolutions. The ending of the birds' debate in *The Owl and the Nightingale* does not prove that the Owl is the 'real' winner, but it is no proof whatever that the Nightingale is genuinely meant to win. The Nightingale may have no right to the victory she claims; she may have won only because she is a nightingale, associated with spring and summer, youth, flowers, and love.[8]

There is, I believe, yet more to be learned about endings. I have stated that the victory of one contestant is no proof of that contestant's fundamental superiority. One can go even further and show that some victories are completely tongue-in-cheek. *Quondam fuit factus festus* (composed in England) offers a very clear example. The narrator sets the scene in a rollicking tone and metre:

Quondam fuit factus festus
et vocatus ad comestus
abbas prior de Leycestris
cum totus familia.

Vinum venit sanguinatis
ad prioris et abbatis.

> nichil nobis paupertatis,
>   sed ad dives omnia.

(stanzas 1,3)

The quarrel flares up when the jovial abbot tells the servants to give some wine to all the monks and the prior demurs. One of the prior's charges, a certain canon, jumps up and denounces him, praying that both abbot and prior might choke to death on their selfishly hoarded wine. A flyting ensues, larded with highly personal insults. Eventually the prior gives in, and wine is distributed. If the poem stopped here, it would only be a poem like *Goliae Dialogus*, with wine, the more pleasant, winning. However, we witness such results as

> Abbas vomit et prioris.
> vomis cadit super floris.
> ego pauper steti foris.
>   et non sum (cum?) leticia.

(stanza 78)

And the poem ends

> Post haec omnes bibierunt
> et in vestes dormierunt,
> matutinas neglexerunt
>   usque ad diem claria a a a etc.

(stanza 102)

Clearly the victory for wine-drinking, far from indicating moral value, is decidedly ironic. This same irony is probably implicit in the usual wine and water debates as well. They are *jeux d'esprit*, meant to amuse the audience because of their refusal to follow an expected didactic line. I doubt that either authors or audience would seriously have defended wine or lover-clerks as the morally proper victors. And indeed some writers on these subjects did dispense with frivolous irony in favour of edification. This observation has no bearing on the Owl's status; it simply offers more evidence that the Nightingale's assertion of victory need not be taken seriously. Other duel poems show quite clearly that irony may be the informing spirit of the conclusion of a debate.

There is one other aspect of the ending which we ought to consider here. The Nightingale's claim to victory appears to be legally correct, so anyone denying her claim must be prepared to explain where her case breaks down. The seed for her victory was planted in lines 1115 ff. There the Nightingale accuses the Owl of being hateful to men when alive and useful to them only after they have killed her. The Nightingale hopes that so damaging a charge will disqualify the Owl in this contest for man's favour. When the Owl gets around to answering (1607 ff.), she does so in more than one way. Immediately before reiterating the charge preparatory to meeting it, she describes at length one instance in which she believes herself to be both useful and *welcome* to humans – she comforts sorrowing women at night:

Hwanne oþre slepeþ hire abute
Ich one lust þar wiðþute,
An wot of hire sore mode,
An singe a niȝt for hire gode:
An mine gode song, for hire þinge,
Ich turne sundel to murni[n]ge.
Of hure seorhe ich bere sume,
Forþan ich am hire wel welcume ...

(1593–1600)

She then restates the Nightingale's original charge and answers it directly:

Þu seist þat ich am manne loð,
An euereuch man is wið me wroð,
An me mid stone & lugge þreteþ,
An me tobusteþ & tobeteþ;
An hwanne heo habeþ me ofslahe
Heo hongeþ me on heore hahe,
Þar ich aschewele pie an crowe
Fron þan þe þar is isowe.
Þah hit beo soþ, ich do heom god
An for heom ich chadde mi blod.

Ich do heom god mid mine deaþe:
Waruore þe is wel unneaþe,
For þah þu ligge dead & clinge
Þi deþ nis naþt to none þinge.
Ich not neauer to hwan þu miȝt,
For þu nart bute a wrecche wiȝt;
Ah þah mi lif me beo atschote,
Þe ȝet ich mai do gode note:
Me mai up one smale sticke
Me sette a wude ine þe þicke,
An swa mai mon tolli him to
Lutle briddes & iuo,
An swa me mai mid me biȝete
Wel gode brede to his mete.
Ah þu neure mon to gode
Liues ne deaþes stal ne stode:
Ich not to hwan þu bretst þi brod,
Liues ne deaþes ne deþ hit god.

(1607–34; italics added)

The elements of her defence are (1) her being welcome to sorrowing women, (2) her counter charge that the Nightingale is useful neither alive nor dead, and (3) her claim to usefulness in death with its heavily biblical overtones.

The climax comes when the Nightingale breaks off the debate, insisting that the Owl boasts of her own shame and is therefore disqualified. By shame she seems principally to mean the Owl's hatefulness to men, but also her being useful only when dead and the shameful mode of her death. The Owl may indeed be hated, though she evidently thinks not ('ich am hire wel welcume' [1600]). But to call her useless when alive is unfair; she helps man however selfishly if only by killing mice. And the death, although unglamorous, is no more shameful than Christ's, which was also technically a punishment for miscreants. The Owl's usefulness to man is not diminished by death, and she has a telling point when she insists that the Nightingale is completely worthless once dead. It seems far from proved that the Owl is boasting of something shameful: that is just the Nightingale's summation, and both birds have shown themselves capable of twisting facts about their opponent in order to score supposed points.[9] Yet even if the Nightingale's charge that the Owl has disqualified herself would stand up in court, the Owl's mistake need not necessarily lose her the case. Atkins, in support of the Nightingale, quotes Pollock and Maitland to the effect that 'Every mistake in pleading, every *miskenning* or *stultiloquium* brought an amercement on the pleader, if the mistake was to be retrieved.'[10] Atkins offers this quotation as evidence that a mistake was very serious, but he ignores the import of the latter half of the statement – *that a mistake could be 'retrieved.'* Even legally the Owl still has some grounds for hope.

One very strong reason for not taking the Nightingale's declaration as final is the birds' obvious belief that the ultimate verdict has not been arrived at. Both feel that Nicholas of Guildford's opinion is necessary for the true winner to be decided. The actual verdict is left completely open. Certainly the Owl does not seem unduly fazed by the Nightingale's triumph; she seems perfectly willing to take the matter to Nicholas, confident that her case is not lost.[11]

The author could easily have made the Nightingale's proclamation convincing had he meant the poem to end decisively. The authors of *The Cuckoo and the Nightingale* and *De Presbytero et Logico* leave no doubts as to how we are meant to rate their contestants, and they work from very similar materials. In all three the winner is declared with the aid of a trick, and in *The Cuckoo and the Nightingale* we also find overt judgment being withheld until the case can be stated before the proper authority. How do these other two authors resolve the ambiguities?

In *De Presbytero et Logico*, a priest and a cocky student start arguing after the student overhears the priest (*obvius sophistæ*) attempting to expound scripture to his flock. When vesper time interrupts their long exchange, they agree that the assembled villagers shall beat the loser, and then they sing the divine offices, the student reading the psalm. As he reads, one line of the psalm sounds like an admission of defeat, and the priest pounces, claiming victory. Unlike the ending of *The Owl and the Nightingale*, the force of this declaration is not dissipated by a deferred judgment. Instead the crowd trounces the student soundly. The Nightingale's cohorts could just as easily have administered a beating to the Owl, and so decisive an action would reinforce the Nightingale's claim and make us take it seriously.

In *The Cuckoo and the Nightingale* the cuckoo withdraws, chased off by the narrator's stone, leaving the nightingale in command of the field. This is obviously a trick-ending whose patent unfairness could have made it easily reversible, particularly as final judgment is deferred until a parliament of birds can convene to judge the dispute. Nonetheless, the nightingale clearly remains the true victor, principally because the narrator favours it so warmly from the outset. *The Owl and the Nightingale* poet could similarly have tipped his hand had he wished either bird to emerge with the advantage. Hence it seems probable that the ending he gives us is not meant to favour one or the other contestant, and the debate cannot be considered 'decided.'

If a critic chooses to ignore the open-endedness of the quarrel, he can find possible grounds for supporting either bird. Nightingale supporters can cite the 'legal' conclusion, the fact that nightingales are not shown elsewhere as losing debates, the generally pleasant associations we have with the bird, and the importance and attractiveness of the human interests they attribute to the Nightingale. Thus Atkins, who values the Nightingale as proponent of the new courtly poetry, sees her winning on all counts. Theoretically, there is no reason why the Nightingale could not win, even if, as Edmund Reiss has argued, the poem was written when victory and defeat were becoming less popular than synthesis as the ending for debates.[12] The other English bird-debates, after all, end in victory for the nightingales yet they were composed later than *The Owl and the Nightingale*, even were it to date from the reign of Henry III or Edward I. In practice, however, there are drawbacks to this interpretation. The Owl's religiosity makes us uneasy at rejecting her. Before the Nightingale may be acclaimed, the critic must prove the Owl's pretensions false. And if the Nightingale is meant to be true victor, why does she seem so hard pressed at times? Why is her pre-eminence not more clear-cut? Why is her logic so faulty when she cites the fable of the cat and the fox, or when she accuses the Owl of vaunting her own shame? A Nightingale supporter has to try to answer questions like these.

If the critic is an Owl supporter, he has to meet similar questions. There is the problem of why the victory is not explicitly accorded to the Owl as it is to the Church or the *croisé*, and why the Nightingale is allowed to gain a technical advantage. Another problem is the Owl's generally unattractive lore. If she is meant to seem genuinely religious,

why do some of her arguments seem to ring false – her claim to exten-
sive knowledge of the scriptures, for instance? Why is she open to the
charge of pride? And why, if she is supposed to be moral, is she so un-
willing to be fair to the Nightingale?

Peterson, one of the most enthusiastic of recent Owl supporters,
argues that *The Owl and the Nightingale* was deliberately left without
explicit resolution in imitation of Abelard's *Sic et Non*, the purpose of
both being to exercise the wits and logical skills of readers.[13] In *The Owl
and the Nightingale*, however, there is no clear statement of what the issue is, an omission which markedly differentiates it from *Sic et Non*
where each proposition is clearly set out at the beginning of its section.
Peterson equates the birds with two 'traditions' or outlooks on life, the
Nightingale's embracing 'sensuality, love, and fertility,' the Owl's 'asceticism, wisdom, and melancholy' (p. 14), and he defines the poem's con-
trolling issue as 'service to mankind.' But if we accept his analysis of the
issue and traditions, we still do not get a *Sic et Non* style of exercise, for
as Peterson defines the two sides, the right answer is self-evident and offers no challenge at all. But these definitions leave something to be de-
sired. Why does he dismiss the Nightingale's claims to religious value
(729–42) and treat her as totally worthless? Is the Owl really being
ruled by Christian wisdom when she swells with rage (143–8), boasts
of her book-learning (1208–12), and says she sympathizes with wives
who, out of anger and spite, commit adultery? In defending them she
seems to be condoning *ira*, one of the deadly sins stemming from 'gostes
custe' not just 'flesches luste' (1397–8). And is the Owl really a respect-
able logician when she asserts '3if ri3t goþ forþ, & abak wrong, / Betere
is mi wop þane þi song' (877–8)? It is perfectly possible to seek truth in
the blistering words of quarrelling fishwives or birds, but the process differs somewhat from that of extracting it from Scripture and the Fathers,
the material Abelard worked with. From fishwives one may divine moral
lessons, but only through a process of extrapolation: one pays less attention to the actual words than to the moral signification of quarrelling.
But when dealing with holy writ one has to take the actual words seriously and deal with them directly. *Sic et Non* and the quodlibetical tradition may be relevant to study of *The Owl and the Nightingale*, but if
so any bearing is indirect, not based on fundamental similarities.

If we neither ignore the end as irrelevant in a plea for preferment nor
support one of the contestants, then logically there is only one approach

left: rating them approximately equal. This can be done in a variety of ways. One is for us to assume the function of judge and reconcile the two, as violet and rose and rose and lily are forcibly reconciled by judge figures. Suzanne Moss Kincaid would have it that we ought to reconcile the two in our minds, for we ought to learn from their quarrel not that they are different, but that they are both part of the divine plan which orders and harmonizes the world.[14] Mortimer J. Donovan suggests that we are meant to rate both as equal because they are really 'good' according to certain traditions, though each thinks her opponent bad on the basis of other traditions.

These critics believe the poem to reflect an optimistic view of the universe, basing this assumption implicitly on the doctrine that whatever is was created by God and therefore is right: consequently they deemphasize the discordant nature of the quarrel. But this assumption is not necessarily correct. The animal world is indeed supposed to be orderly, but these birds seem to partake enough in man's nature to share some of man's faults. Hence another school of critics concentrates with at least equal validity on the birds' flaws. Wells and Kinneavy suggest that we are meant to deduce and accept an outlook on life which lies between those of the two birds, combining the virtues of both while avoiding their vices. Still another possibility would be to view both birds' outlooks as viable and useful when purged of their particular exponents' faults. Although I believe that neither bird is meant to win, the precise manner in which they are meant to be balanced remains to be found.

In this chapter, I have surveyed the nature of *The Owl and the Nightingale*'s form against the background of medieval literary debates, hoping to clarify the interpretative issues which spring from the poem's problematical conclusion. Three points emerge. (1) Non-human protagonists normally debate non-intellectual issues, and if they speak on serious subjects, it is directly (as in *The Thrush and the Nightingale*), not obliquely through the disguise of animal concerns. (2) The Nightingale's technical victory is suitable, both because she is the pleasanter debater in a lighthearted poem, and because she is a perennially popular bird not elsewhere defeated. (3) By looking at the ironies and moralities of other endings, we can recognize the intellectual and even the legal insubstantiality of the Nightingale's self-proclaimed victory.

The most interesting of these points is the conclusion that a poem of this sort is not usually the vehicle for serious, extended commentary on important human issues. Because this observation plainly runs counter to many recent interpretations, it needs to be scrutinized with particular care. Intellectual and religious issues are often said to be significant, even central, in the birds' quarrel. In the next chapter I propose to investigate the presence of such issues and try to assess their importance.

NOTES

1 For the historical background of the debate form, see James Holly Hanford, 'Classical Eclogue and Mediæval Debate' *Romanic Review* 2 (1911) 16–31, 129–43; and F.J.E. Raby, *A History of Secular Latin Poetry in the Middle Ages*, 2nd ed., 2 vols. (Oxford: Clarendon Press 1957) II 282–308; and H. Walther, *Das Streitgedicht in der lateinischen Literatur des Mittelalters*, Quellen und Untersuchungen zur Lateinischen Philologie des Mittelalters, vol. 5, part 2 (Munich: C.H. Beck'sche 1920).

2 For Alcuin's *Conflictus Veris et Hiemis*, see *Monumenta Germaniae Historica, Poetae Latini Aevi Carolini*, ed. E. Duemmler and others, 4 vols. (Berlin: Weidmahnsche 1881 on) I 270–2; for the *Carmen Nigelli Ermoldi Exulis in Laudem Gloriosissimi Pippini Regis*, see vol. II of the same work (1884), pp. 79–85; for Sedulius Scotus' *De Rosae Liliique Certamine*, see vol. III (1896), pp. 230–1; and for Theodulus' *Eclogue* see *Theoduli eclogam recensuit et prolegomenis instruxit prof. Dr. Joannes Osternacher* (Ripariae prope Lentiam: Collegium Petrinum 1902).

3 These debates may be consulted in the following editions. Walther's *Das Streitgedicht* contains the *Discussio litis super hereditate Lazari et Marie Magdalene, sororis eius, videlicet quis eorum debeat habere eorum hereditatem*. The various clerk-knight debates, both Latin and French, have been edited by Charles Oulmont in his *Les Débats du clerc et du Chevalier*. *The Latin Poems commonly attributed to Walter Mapes*, ed. Thomas Wright (London: printed for the Camden Society by J.B. Nichols and Son 1841) contains an assortment of debates including *De Clarevallensibus et Cluniacensibus*, *De Presbytero et Logico*, and *De Mauro et Zoilo*. *Nouveau Recueil de Contes, Dits, Fabliaux et autre pièces inédites des xiiie, xive et xve siècles*, ed. Achille Jubinal, 2 vols. (Paris: É. Pannier 1839; Challamel 1842) contains various French debates including *Marguet Convertie*. *Altercatio Rusticorum et Clericorum* was edited by W. Wattenbach in *Anzeiger für Kunde der deutschen Vorzeit* 24 (1877) cols. 369–72. *Quondam fuit factus festus*, ed. Wilhelm Meyer, appears in *Nachrichten von der Königlichen Gesellschaft der Wissenschaften zu Göttingen* (Berlin: Weidmannsche 1908) 406–26. And *De Ganymede et Helena*, edited by W. Wattenbach, appears in *ZfdA* 18 (1875) 124–36.

4 Some debaters like the seasons or Youth and Age are clearly not real persons, though they often parade in human form. I have chosen to stress the innate nature of the opposition, not the external shape, by classifying these as I have. Winner and Waster could be classified either way. In the clerk-knight debates

human contestants give way to avian champions, but it is the humans who determine the debate's subject. Debates between parts of the body (Heart and
Eye, for instance) or Spirit and Flesh centre on moral issues; though this makes
them exceptions to the rule that non-humans debate non-intellectual issues, the
reasons for the aberration are so obvious that they constitute no serious challenge to that generalization.

5 The *Conflictus Ovis et Lini*, edited by M. Haupt, appears in *ZfdA* 11 (1859)
215-38. For bibliographic information on all of the wine and water debates,
see James Holly Hanford, 'The Mediæval Debate between Wine and Water'
PMLA 28 (1913) 315-67. Among the most important versions, the *Goliae
Dialogus* and the *Desputoison du Vin et de l'Iaue* can be found in Wright, and
the *Denudata Veritate* in *Carmina Burana*, ed. J.A. Schmeller (Stuttgart: K. Fr.
Hering 1847) no. 173. *The Violet and the Rose*, ed. Adolf Tobler, appears in
Archiv 90 (1893) 152-8. *Le Petit Plet* has been edited by Brian S. Merrilees,
Anglo-Norman Text Society 20 (Oxford: Basil Blackwell 1970).

6 In Sedulius' *Certamen*, for example, the flowers both praise their own beauty
and deride the other's looks as do the Owl and Nightingale, in phrases like

> *Rose*
> Purpura dat regnum, fit purpura gloria regni;
> Regibus ingrato vilescunt alba colore.
>
> (5-6)
>
> *Lily*
> Me decus auricomum telluris pulcher Apollo
> Diligit ac niveo faciem vestivit honore.
>
> (9-10)

The lily taunts the rose about her thorns:

> Nam diadema tui spinis terebratur acutis:
> Eheu – quam miserum laniant spineta rosetum.
>
> (19-20)

And the rose defends these ambivalent features (as does the Owl her claws and
love of darkness) as part of her God-given nature:

> Conditor omnicreans spina me sepsit acuta,
> Muniit et roseos praeclaro tegmine vultus.
>
> (23-4)

Spring orders the squabbling flowers to make up their quarrel, and points out
the virtues of both:

> Tu, rosa, martyribus rutilam das stemmate palmam,
> Lilia, virgineas turbas decorate stolatas.
>
> (41-2)

7 Versions of the Church-Synagogue and Christian-Jew dispute are listed by
Margaret Schlauch in 'The Allegory of Church and Synagogue' *Speculum* 14
(1939) 448–64. Rutebeuf's *La Desputaison du Croisé et du Décroisé* appears
in *Œuvres Complètes de Rutebeuf*, ed. Edmond Faral and Julia Bastin, 2 vols.
(Paris: A. et J. Picard et Cie 1959, 1960) I 470–8. The disputants are one who
has taken the cross to go on a crusade and one who has not.

8 There may even be a tradition protecting nightingales from defeat. In all the
clerk-knight debates but *Le Geste de Blancheflour e de Florence*, the clerk's
champion is a nightingale, and it triumphs. In *le geste*, however, the clerk supporters are defeated, and in this version, the nightingale is replaced by the less-
beloved lark. In the fifteenth-century fragment known as *The Clerk and the
Nightingale II*, the nightingale acts as if she has triumphed over a human contestant. (See Rossell Hope Robbins, *Secular Lyrics of the XIVth and XVth
Centuries*, 2nd ed. [Oxford: Clarendon Press 1955] 176–9.)

9 Stanley, p. 27, defines the crux as follows: 'the subject of the birds' dispute is,
strictly speaking, the usefulness of their existence; but death is the end of existence, and it is, so the Nightingale pleads, only in death that the Owl is useful to
mankind.' This is a clear explication of the Nightingale's viewpoint, but I do
not see the justification for limiting our interest to life alone. The Nightingale,
of course, wants to discredit usefulness after death because she can lay claim
to none, but that does not mean that her view is fair.

10 Atkins, p. liv; Pollock and Maitland, *History of English Law* II 519

11 M. Angela Carson, in 'Rhetorical Structure in *The Owl and the Nightingale*'
Speculum 42 (1967) 92–103, has argued that the Owl is even more confident
of Nicholas of Guildford's favour than the Nightingale. She insists that the
Nightingale's feeble protest (1745–9) that she does not know where Nicholas
lives is an 'attempt to evade formal decision of Nicholas' (p. 102) because she
knows it will go against her.

12 'Conflict and its Resolution in Medieval Dialogues' in *Arts Libéraux et Philosophie au Moyen Âge*, Actes du quatrième Congrès international de Philosophie
médiévale (Montreal and Paris, 1969) 863–72

13 Douglas L. Peterson '*The Owl and the Nightingale* and Christian Dialectic'
JEGP 55 (1956) 13–26. *Sic et Non* is found in *PL* 178, cols. 1339–1610.

14 For Kincaid's views, see pp. 130 and 205 of 'The Art of *The Owl and the
Nightingale*.'

4
intellectual
and religious
interpretations

What is *The Owl and the Nightingale* really about? In 1948 Albert C.
Baugh denied that the poem was 'anything more than a lively altercation
between two birds,'[1] and almost every critic since has gone out of his way
to protest this assessment. And it *is* difficult to believe that a poem of
such length and quality should be merely a *jeu d'esprit*. Failure to see its
meaning has driven critics to try explaining the poem by means of external contexts; in other words, to reading it allegorically. My object in this
chapter and the next is to weigh the usefulness of this approach, starting
with the readings which build on issues mentioned in the text (music,
astrology) and moving to those which treat the work as an *à clef* composition. The question is what kind of reading the poem demands. Must the
audience extrapolate to allegorical referents to make sense of the work?
Is the poem naturally suited to this approach? Can we hope the poem
will yield to allegorical assault in the future if past attempts have failed?

The most common and least allegorical of the usual approaches is that
which tries to explain the poem in terms of 'outlook on life.' The birds'
outlooks have been classified as 'beauty, brilliancy, youth, cheerfulness'
for the Nightingale, and 'serious, gloomy, sullen old age' for the Owl, or
pleasure and asceticism (both descriptions are Ten Brink's); gaiety and
gravity (Saintsbury); Art and Philosophy (W.P. Ker); joyous and solemn
(Stanley); and aesthetic and serious (Wells).[2] Though these terms reflect
differing emphases, the nature of the dichotomy discerned by these critics is clear: essentially it is a contrast between gloom and joy, modified
by those human interests which the critic thinks to be involved allegorically; thus the Owl's gloom is not mere sourness, but is linked by several

critics to religious asceticism. Because evidence of this dichotomy is so important to most interpretations, it is worth examining in some detail.

The difference in outlook suggested by the birds' perches – the flowering spray and the ivy-covered tree-trunk – is confirmed by what we learn of their natural traits and lore. The Owl, for example, is not just a denizen of the dark; she is associated with emotional darkness – sorrow. The Nightingale makes this clear:

> Þu singist a niȝt & noȝt a dai,
> & al þi song is "wailawai".
> Þu miȝt mid þine songe afere
> Alle þat ihereþ þine ibere.
> Þu schirchest & ȝollest to þine fere
> Þat hit is grislich to ihere.
> Hit þincheþ boþe wise & snepe,
> Noȝt þat þu singe, ac þat þu wepe.
>
> (219–26)

The Owl agrees that she sings at night, but tries to reinterpret the fact as reflecting quasi priestly or monkish status. The Nightingale accuses the Owl of being unwelcome, disparages the times she sings, and blames her for malicious destruction of men's happiness (411–32), but the Owl has good answers (473–84). Her subsequent condemnation of the Nightingale's cheerful activities is reminiscent of the gloomy disapproval towards worldly joy expressed by religious ascetics. The birds' association with religion is made explicit when they disagree over how man can best prepare for heaven. The Owl says:

> Þu seist þat þu singist mankunne,
> & techest hom þat hi fundieþ honne
> Vp to þe songe þat eure ilest.
> Ac hit is alre wnder mest
> Þat þu darst liȝe so opeliche.
> Wenest þu hi bringe so liȝtliche
> To Godes riche al singinge?
> Nai, nai, hi shulle wel auinde

Þat hi mid longe wope mote
Of hore sunnen bidde bote,
Ar hi mote euer kume þare.
Ich rede þi þat men bo ȝare
An more wepe þane singe,
Þat fundeþ to þan houenkinge ...
Mid mine songe ich hine pulte,
Þat he groni for his gulte.

(849–62, 873–4)

Such passages explain the Owl's reputation for gravity, and the many identifications of her as religious ascetic, moralist, and philosopher.

The Nightingale's character is similarly projected with the help of natural history, lore, and emotional associations. Physically she is linked to flowers, and her song to cheerful music from pipe and harp (22). She describes her own role in glowing terms:

Ac ich alle blisse mid me bringe,
Ech wiȝt is glad for mine þinge
& blisseþ hit wanne ich cume,
& hiȝteþ aȝen mine kume.
Þe blostme ginneþ springe & sprede,
Boþe ine tro & ek on mede.
Þe lilie mid hire faire wlite
Wolcumeþ me – þat þu hit w[i]te! –
Bid me mid hire faire blo
Þat ich shulle to hire flo.
Þe rose also, mid hire rude
Þat cumeþ ut of þe þornevvode,
Bit me þat ich shulle singe
Vor hire luue one skentinge.
& ich so do þurȝ niȝt & dai –
Þe more ich singe þe more i mai –
An skente hi mid mine songe,
Ac noþeles noȝt ouerlonge ...

(433–50)

The Owl, however, adds her own interpretation:

Vor sumeres tide is al to wlonc
An doþ misreken monnes þonk;
Vor he ne recþ noȝt of clennesse,
Al his þoȝt is of golnesse ...
& þu sulf art þaramong,
For of golnesse is al þi song,
An aȝen þet þu vvlt teme
Þu art wel modi & wel breme.
Sone so þu hauest itrede
Ne miȝtu leng a word iqueþe ...
A sumere chorles awedeþ
& uorcrempeþ & uorbredeþ.
Hit nis for luue noþeles,
Ac is þe chorles wode res;
Vor wane he haueþ ido his dede
Ifallen is al his boldhede;
Habbe he istunge under gore
Ne last his luue no leng more.
Also hit is on þine mode:
So sone so þu sittest a brode
Þu forlost al þine wise.
Also þu farest on þine rise:
Wane þu hauest ido þi gome
Þi steune goþ anon to shome.

(489–92, 497–502, 509–22)

The Nightingale emerges from this attack with an undeniable tie to love
and sexuality, while the Owl's prurient insistence on the lust-provoking
qualities of the Nightingale's song links her to a religious-ascetic viewpoint.

The Nightingale's views on how man can best get to heaven are also
important to our understanding of her character:

Wostu to wan man was ibore? –
To þare blisse of houene riche,

Þar euer is song & murȝþe iliche;
Þider fundeþ eurich man
Þat eni þing of gode kan.
Vorþi me singþ in holi chirche
An clerkes ginneþ songes wirche,
Þat man iþenche bi þe songe
Wider he shal, & þar bon longe;
Þat he þe murȝþe ne uorȝete,
Ac þarof þenche & biȝete,
An nime ȝeme of chirche steuene
Hu murie is þe blisse of houene.

(716–28)

Clearly there is good cause to think of the Nightingale as interested in pleasure, gaiety, art, joy, aesthetics, sex, and perhaps in the sort of 'new' religion based on love and joy that was popularized by the Franciscans.

With this evidence before us, we can readily understand why so many critics have interpreted the poem as a conflict between some type of joy and gloom. This approach has the considerable virtue that it demands almost no extension beyond the text. We may extrapolate from such indirect statements as the Owl's periodic night songs to the canonical hours if we wish to add a religious touch, but that is hardly a great leap. The birds' comments on human concerns like adultery surely warrant our assuming there is some connection between them and man.

One substantial objection to general-outlook interpretations, however, is the peripheral placement of the evidence. Virtually all of it appears in the first half of the poem, much indeed before line 500. As the arguments unfold, it becomes clear that the controversy centres on service to mankind, and outlook proves of little relevance to the points scored or issues discussed. Indeed, the outlooks seem at odds with the birds' later pronouncements on astrology and fornication. Arrangement of the evidence in this fashion suggests that details about outlook, many of which are extensions of bird lore, were used to endow the birds with personality, not to define the meaning of the whole debate.

Another objection to interpreting the poem by outlook is our inability to equate the birds with consistent human philosophies. The Owl's characterization is straightforward: she represents all that is conservative, ascetic, and solemn, and may readily be labelled priest, philosopher, or monk.[3] Handling the Nightingale in the same fashion though, translating her traits and actions into human terms, results in a contradiction: half of her personality establishes her as secular opposition to the Owl; her strong connection with sexual love and her defence of maidens who slip make her seem a lay figure. But her claims to helping clergy of various descriptions (729–42) and her theological opinions on how to get to heaven designate her as a 'new' religious figure of the Franciscan or proto-Franciscan type. This duality greatly reduces our hope of identifying her with a consistent human stance, and with that any hope of interpreting the poem solely by means of outlook. One might also question whether female birds would have been chosen to represent serious religious philosophies.[4]

The contradictions inherent in the characterization of the Nightingale seem to me clearest evidence that this debate is not an exploration of two outlooks or philosophies of life. Such an approach leaves too much of the poem out of account; many an avian detail cannot be translated into human terms, and many subjects such as astrology and sexual lapses seem ill-suited to this interpretation of the birds. And since the work's focus shifts from personality to serving mankind, we cannot dismiss the poem as a simple confrontation for confrontation's sake like the quarrels between seasons. We can only conclude that outlooks are of secondary importance, not the key to the poem.

Since study of the birds' philosophies of life does not tell us what *The Owl and the Nightingale* is about, critics have attempted to find out by examining the issues debated. Some, attempting to avoid allegoresis as much as possible, have combed the text for commentary on any issue which might seem substantial enough to pass for the subject of the whole. Though the kaleidoscopic nature of the arguments discourages such approaches, two have been put forward: Bertram Colgrave proposes music as the theme, and A.C. Cawley astrology.[5]

Colgrave's argument can be broken into three contentions: (1) that the debate concerns musical practices; (2) that the Owl and the Nightingale represent respectively Gregorian chant and troubadour-influenced music; and (3) that the good man from Rome is John the Archchanter, who went to England about 680 to teach the barbarian Englishmen how to sing Gregorian music. The first is simply not adequate. It builds on a relatively small portion of the text, and ignores a great number of other issues. Gloom, joy, lechery, and romantic love all have some relevance to a discussion of music, but the birds' diets and nesting habits do not. Neither do the references to astrology or the Owl's crucifixion. Singing may be *an* issue, but it is not *the* issue. Colgrave's identification of the birds is equally questionable. He ignores the fact that the Owl helps men sing *conduts* at Christmas (481-4), yet the *condut* or *conductus* is a motet based, by definition, on a *non*-Gregorian melody. As for the man from Rome, Colgrave's identification contradicts his own contentions. The Nightingale says (1015-20) that this mysterious figure taught northerners good customs, which Colgrave interprets as 'good music,' but the music John the Archchanter taught was Gregorian plainsong, the very type of music the Nightingale is supposedly trying to argue down in the figure of the Owl! All in all, this attempt to interpret the poem as a treatise on singing seems unconvincing.

A.C. Cawley, working outward from some intriguing observations on the specific meaning of the prophecy passage (1145-1330), suggests that the poem is about astrology. The Nightingale has the 'traditionally hostile attitude of the Church towards astrology' while the Owl seems to be something like an 'apologist of a Christianized astrology.' Each of the disasters mentioned by the birds is indeed attributable to one of the malign planets, and Cawley's observations on this material are fascinating. It is unfortunate for his argument though that the Owl never cites the stars as her source of information; nor does the Nightingale seem to think astrology nonsense: 'Ich habbe iherd, & soþ hit is, / Þe mon mot beo wel storrewis' (1317-18). She is merely denying that the Owl can read stars meaningfully, and accuses her of prophesying by means of witchcraft (1301).

Laying this objection aside for a minute, though, we can assess the interpretation's general utility. It explains the Owl quite as adequately as any other reading: her liking for darkness befits a star-gazer; her mournful 'wailawai' is appropriate for conveying warning of disasters. The Nightingale though resists identification as usual. Her cheer, the welcome flowers give her, her connection with sex, are all irrelevant to any stand on astrology she may care to take, and so are details of diet and nest sanitation. Though the Owl can be linked to astrology in general, and the Nightingale to Venus, there is nothing in the Nightingale's chief characteristics to motivate her hostility to astrology, and on these grounds I think Cawley's general reading breaks down.

Cawley and Colgrave confine their attentions to issues mentioned directly in the poem, and can be said to read allegorically only in so far as they translate the birds' comments on music and astrological prophecy into human terms. The other principal subject to be mentioned directly – the birds' relative usefulness to mankind – has rarely seemed important enough to constitute the *raison d'être* of so long a poem. It is no wonder therefore that a more elaborately allegorical approach has attracted so many critics.

Atkins and Owst appear, at first glance, to have worked along lines similar to Colgrave's, but they interpret the poem in terms of completely allegorical referents, not issues mentioned in the text. They take a poem dealing with birds' appearances, birdsong, bird diets, nest building, and birds' deaths (with human adultery and astrology thrown in) and say, in effect, 'Aha! Obviously this all has to do with old didactic and new courtly poetry writing' (Atkins) or 'old thunderous and new joyous preaching' (Owst). These are rather long leaps, though in fairness we must admit that they are not impossible.

Atkins identifies the Owl as the gloomy defender of didactic poetry, the Nightingale as the cheerful lay defender of the new courtly, secular poetry. He depends for evidence on all the passages concerning singing, working on the hypothesis that singing is to birds what poetry is to man. His approach explains the Owl no better than do those of Colgrave and Owst: in all three she emerges as the defender of the old and gloomy, be it music, preaching, or poetry. But in its ability to handle the Nightingale, Atkins's view has much to recommend it. Her habit of singing outside bowers where lords and ladies are in bed can be explained as a reflection of courtly poetry's concern with the love affairs of the highborn. So can her participation in the clash between the jealous knight and his wife, a role played by a nightingale in one of Marie de France's most courtly lais. Her unwillingness to sing in northern countries, which is a natural fact but is treated as a matter of choice, can be explained as her knowing that there was no courtly culture in the north and hence no place for her.[6]

Furthermore Atkins's approach has one advantage which no other can match: we can feel certain that the author of *The Owl and the Nightingale* did have some interest in poetry writing. Whether he loved music or was tone deaf, was stirred by one type of sermon or another, we can never know. But he *must* have been interested in secular poetry or presumably he never would have written such a long specimen. His, indeed, is one of the very few poems not overtly didactic to have been preserved from the pre-Chaucerian age.

But the disadvantage in this interpretation is that, like all the other single-theme theories, it does not account satisfactorily for all the turns the birds' arguments take. Astrology and prophecy lie outside such an explanation, as do all passages related to the protagonists as birds. Nor is there any direct connection between the Owl's crucifixion and didactic poetry. Inevitably, with this approach, we stumble over the irreducibly avian part of the poem which will not adapt itself to intellectual issues.

Do we gain any more satisfying insights by trying to explain the debate in terms of preaching techniques? G.R. Owst has suggested the possibility, though he does not explore it in depth:

> Perhaps no modern commentator yet has hit upon the real significance of that remarkable Old-English poem known as *The Owl and the Nightingale.* Is it not, after all, intended to be an allegory of the age-long rivalry in the preaching of medieval Christendom between those who upheld the gentler themes of love and bliss and an ever-forgiving Redeemer, and those who preferred on the other hand to thunder of sin and Judgment and the Wrath to come? There is certainly evidence that this very problem was continually weighing upon the minds of contemporary churchmen. In the pulpits, at all events, the note of the Owl is heard most often.[7]

The lines which suggest this reading constitute a substantial part of the poem, but not all of it. Like other single-theme interpretations, this one has trouble encompassing all of the issues raised. Again, astrology and adultery do not fit, nor do such details of avian life as diet and nest-construction. It is to the credit of these critics that they do not desperately twist the poem to make it agree with their constructs, but this honesty only makes clearer the weaknesses of this type of approach.

Given such explicit references to religion in the poem and the upsurge of critical interest in the effect religion had on medieval literature, it comes as no surprise that critics have tried to illuminate *The Owl and the Nightingale* by referring it to a religious context.[8]

Robertson's treatment, though sketchy, has been influential. He identifies the contestants as Christian wisdom and fleshly love, using the same evidence which has attracted other critics. He buttresses his argument with such details as the Owl's ivied stump, which supposedly represents everlasting life, and the Nightingale's flowering spray, which is the flesh that is grass and withers, the beautiful but perishable things of the world. The Owl proves her wisdom by resisting the Nightingale's siren song – she refuses to be snared by delusions, she keeps in mind the last things and is not seduced to improper pleasures.

Nightingale supporters would like to reject so unfavourably sensual an interpretation of her activities as warped, but the evidence is hard to dismiss altogether. The Nightingale admits that it is her custom to sing outside the bower window when a lord takes his lady to bed. Indeed, she asserts, 'Hit is mi riȝt, hit is mi laȝe / Þat to þe hexst ich me draȝe' (969–70). And when the Owl accuses the Nightingale of leading maidens into carnal transgressions with her song, the Nightingale denies that she encourages such falls, and insists that the Owl misinterprets the relationship between her song and love, but she cannot deny that there is a connection between them. Though the Nightingale obviously does not consider herself an exponent of near-heretical sensuality, she has potentially compromising ties to it.

Herbert Hässler identifies the Nightingale with the philosophical stance he labels 'natural man,' comprising elements of Ailred of Rievaulx's neoplatonism, elements of high courtliness, courtly love, and courtly poetry. The Owl he equates with a religious ascetic stance. His view of the birds' relative merits coincides with Robertson's: the Owl is morally superior, the Nightingale attractive but useless:

> Die Dichtung der Nachtigall besteht eben nur aus einer reizvollen Hülle ohne jeden tieferen Kern, da sie nicht aus der Quelle göttlicher Wahrheit schöpft, aus der die theologische Vertreterin ihre Werke bereichert (p. 160).

Moreover, both men seem to assume that the point of the poem is a conflict between right and wrong. There are medieval debates with no more meaning than that – Church and Synagogue or *The Merle and the Nychtingaill* – but all such works grant utterly unambiguous victory to the defender of the right. If *The Owl and the Nightingale* is the sort of work these men implicitly assume it to be, why is the Owl not shown winning?

When we turn to Peterson and Donovan, we find that they too are more concerned with identifying the birds than with the poem's overall purpose, with similar detriment to their theories. Peterson, who identifies the birds as Robertson does, posits that the whole point to the poem is the listener's attempting to evaluate the birds. But since, according to the evidence he relies on, this could be accomplished by line 900 at the very latest, we would expect audience-interest to have dried up half-way through. And as usual, certain issues the birds argue over do not fit into his reading: adultery, a subject which *should* be highly significant in a conflict between sensuality and wisdom, does not accord with his scheme – the Owl is too lenient for one of her ascetic views. He explains the Owl's forgiving attitude as reflecting Abelardian concern for intention and circumstances, but it can be argued that the offending wives commit adultery out of spite and anger. The Owl's logic here may be no better than the Nightingale's.

Donovan, as I noted in Chapter 2, starts with the patristic information available and to some extent used by the other three, yet he concludes that the poem is a display of mistaken identities: the Nightingale believes the Owl to be all that is bad in her lore, whereas she is really all that is good; likewise, the Owl mistakes the Nightingale for a songster of carnal love whereas she is really a chorister of divine praise. Aside from the fact that different conclusions can be drawn from the same patristic lore, a further drawback to its use is its relative abstruseness. Few of the author's auditors are likely to have been as well up on the niceties of biblical exegesis as Donovan, especially since the poem is written in English, not Latin. His elaborate explication may be slightly beside the point if the poem was read aloud to a group which had to take its cues from the text and deduce from the Owl's overt religiosity that her claims were to be accorded some credence. In favour of Donovan's approach however is its ability to encompass all the avian details: his theory is firmly grounded in acceptance of the protagonists as birds, not just projections of human abstractions.

Although there is more agreement among Hässler, Robertson, and Peterson than in any other group of critics (excepting those who settle for the general-outlook theory), their interpretations are not without serious drawbacks. And since Donovan worked with the same material but came up with a very different result, we cannot but feel that these attempts were not properly tested.

The characters which the author has bestowed on his protagonists are maddeningly suggestive. They are different enough to imply that he had a specific human dichotomy in mind, yet not so specific and individualized that we can be sure of the referents. Because a dichotomy is obviously present, critics have tried to relate it to medieval struggles of all kinds. But this game is all too easy. Choosing at random among possibilities that spring to mind, I can set up quite a promising case for identifying the Nightingale as a student-clerk, the Owl as a conservative priest, rather like the protagonists in *De Presbytero et Logico*. As there, it is the cocky student who precipitates the quarrel, challenging the old-fashioned figure of authority. The birds in these capacities could be made out to argue over the sorts of lessons they teach, the Owl preferring the preaching of repentance, the student the intoxicating pleasure and power of dialectic. The Nightingale sees in the Owl only a gloomy old stick-in-the-mud, out of touch with all current intellectual concerns. The Owl finds the Nightingale a dangerous radical, whose shameless curiosity and presumption is the sort which leads men to defile the holy Trinity by attempting to strip it of its mystery with logical analysis 'like a shop-keeper peeling an onion.' The student has no interest in going to the far north – there are no universities there, no stimulating discussion of universals. The Owl, however, must preach in such far reaches of Christendom, despite their lack of amenities, and therefore feels somewhat jealous of the student's avoidance of this sort of drudgery and suffering. The Owl sings the canonical hours faithfully. The Nightingale claims to aid others to sing them; this may reflect the method of performing Low Mass, which was normally carried out by a priest aided by one clerk, as is the Vesper service in *De Presbytero et Logico*. The Nightingale's interest in sex could be taken as referring to bawdy Goliardic student verse, as well as to the courtly poetry which such a clerk might appreciate more fully than this moralistic priest would. The link between Nightingale and sex could also refer to student sexual mores. When the Nightingale curses the Owl, calling on God and all that wear linen cloth to hate her, the Owl-priest might well challenge the right of a mere clerk to call down God's wrath.

Surely this sketch is not much less plausible than the interpretations of other scholars. Like most of their attempts, this one describes personages who would, by profession, agree in general outlook with the birds, and it fits as many portions of the debate into the interpretation as will go but ignores those that will not. The Owl's crucifixion does not fit; neither do the birds' menus or the astrological passages.

Or one might set up another construct – and I have heard this one upheld informally – that had the poem been composed later, it would *have* to be about monks and friars. This critic was working on the old dating assumptions, but let us examine the possibility for a moment, remembering that both manuscripts could date from as late as 1275. The Owl is a perfect monk, singing canonical hours, taking the appropriate view of how to get to heaven, even (possibly) wearing the white of the Cistercian order. The Nightingale is an equally perfect friar after the manner of St Francis. She believes in love, joy, and song, not gloomy weeping. Friars were the famous, energetic, and influential proponents of joy-oriented preaching; the Owl's preference is obviously for the older, hell-fire and brimstone type of sermonizing, and for the floods of tears which Pope Gregory the Great commended. The Nightingale's claim to religious value (which does not fit theories in which she is identified with lay concerns) fits this interpretation perfectly. All in all, this approach looks promising.

But consider: if the poem was written any time between 1180 and 1200, it almost certainly does not refer to the Franciscans, for Francis was only born in 1181 or 1182, and the order was not given its papally approved rules until 1223. If it was written after friars became widely recognized, why are they never mentioned in the poem? The Nightingale refers to 'clerkes, munekes & kanunes' and 'prostes' (729, 733), and elsewhere in the poem bishops and the pope are mentioned, but not friars. It seems unlikely that the Nightingale would not overtly ally herself with them in 729 ff. even as the Owl aligns herself with monks in 323 ff., if monks and friars were the 'real' debaters. Thus one more promising dichotomy fails to stand up to scrutiny.

Of all the intellectual contexts suggested thus far, none fits perfectly, and none is capable of subsuming the masses of purely avian detail. Unless some fantastic mass blindness has afflicted all critics to the present, it seems unlikely that anyone will present an intellectual frame never before considered, and find it to be just what scholars have always been seeking. Not that there is any insuperable theoretical objection to allegory. But continued attempts to leave the text and find its meaning outside have failed. Under the circumstances, unless a hitherto unnoticed context presents itself, it is probably wiser to stick to what we have:

there is really no point to yet another procrustean attempt to make the text congruent with an allegory by lopping off the extremities or stretching and twisting until the two levels coincide.

Another reason for being chary of allegorical interpretations is the nature of the form. A survey of debates of all sorts in the last chapter uncovered no evidence that would lead us to expect the birds' exchanges to be serious and extended commentary on a single issue of import to mankind. Furthermore, most medieval allegories are more obviously just that than *The Owl and the Nightingale.* Not until *Parliament of Fowls*, written one or two centuries later, do we find a piece whose issues are as hard to separate from the colourful surface, and even there we do have ample evidence that the basic subject is love. The diversity of proposed allegorical interpretations of *The Owl and the Nightingale* shows just how unsure we are of what the poem's subject really is. Complete obscurity of the central point is not typical of serious intellectual endeavours in any age, modern or medieval, particularly when the author's problem is so clearly not one of expression.

Critics have striven to transcend the earthy texture of the poem, hoping to find an orderly intellectual framework which will explain and clarify a peculiarly teasing text. But the very difficulties encountered – not to mention the diversity of the results – should suggest that an allegorical solution is unlikely. What sane man, endowed with such skill of expression, would set out to write a serious intellectual treatise and give it such a vehicle? The two birds are emotional, flighty, erratic, and irrational – charming creatures engrossed in their lore, characters, and squabbles. Their vivid and pervasive presence makes much of the poem seem irreducibly avian. If the birds' quarrel was conceived merely as a vehicle for a treatise on preaching or poetry writing, then the poet failed miserably, since expert readers cannot agree on what his subject really was. It seems more likely that the problem lies less in the poem than in the readers who insist on looking for a kind of meaning which the work simply does not contain.

NOTES

1 Albert C. Baugh, general editor and author of the Middle English portion, *A Literary History of England*, 2nd ed. (New York: Appleton-Century-Crofts 1967) 155

2 Ten Brink, p. 215; George Saintsbury, *A Short History of English Literature* (New York: Macmillan 1898) 60; W.P. Ker, *Medieval English Literature* (1912; reprint, London: Oxford University Press 1962) 135; Stanley, p. 22; and Wells, p. xli

3 The Owl's views on wives' adultery are not altogether in line with her austere characterization, although most readers welcome this lapse in logic for the humanity it signifies. If the Owl is meant to be a monk – and this is the most usual identification – we may be able to go further and call her a Cistercian. Hinckley (in *PMLA* [1932] 304) points out that we may deduce the Owl to be white from her disparagement of the Nightingale for her dusky coloration (577 ff.). But, of course, the birds accuse each other of faults they themselves share: the Nightingale, for example, loudly berates the Owl over her diet, only to be proven far from fastidious herself.

4 Their sex may reflect linguistic rather than physical gender, as seems to be the case with the falcon, so it is unsafe to base an interpretation on that characteristic.

5 Bertram Colgrave, '*The Owl and the Nightingale* and the "Good Man from Rome"' *ELN* 4 (1966) 1–4; and A.C. Cawley, 'Astrology in "The Owl and the Nightingale"' *MLR* 46 (1951) 161–74. Richard E. Allen, in 'The Voices of *The Owl and the Nightingale*' (*Studies in Medieval Culture* 3 [1970] 52–8) supports Colgrave's musical interpretation throughout most of his argument, but suggests as a further possibility a connection to epic and romance.

6 Norway, for instance, was eventually to embrace courtly works, but the stirrings of interest in that sort of literature in the north are not documented until 1226 when King Hakon ordered translated the Tristram story and then Marie's lais.

7 *Literature and Pulpit in Medieval England*, 2nd ed. (Oxford: Basil Blackwell 1961) 22

8 D.W. Robertson's essay, only incidentally on *The Owl and the Nightingale*, is 'Historical Criticism' in *English Institute Essays 1950*, ed. Alan S. Downer (1951; reprint New York: AMS Press 1965) 3–31, especially pp. 23–6. Hässler's views are expressed in '*The Owl and the Nightingale*' *und die literarischen Bestrebungen des 12. und 13. Jahrhunderts* (Frankfurt 1942?). Peterson's and Donovan's essays appeared simultaneously in 1956 in *JEGP* and *MS* respectively.

historical and political interpretations

Although the objections I have raised to intellectual allegory apply in part to political allegory as well, a fundamental difference between the two forms must be acknowledged. I am not investigating political and historical contexts merely for the pleasure of beating a dead horse. A writer may allegorize intellectual issues for various reasons – to sugar-coat his instructive pill, to provide a pleasant exercise for his readers' wits, or to make a lesson more vivid – but the process of veiling is certainly not undertaken in order to obscure the author's message. A political writer, in sharp contradistinction, may well allegorize for the express purpose of partially obscuring his referents. Those in the know will understand, but the writer runs less risk of affronting his butts than he would by criticizing them directly. Political allegories are generally *à clef* compositions: at no point, for example, does Dryden's *Absalom and Achitophel* refer to any but biblical events. If *The Owl and the Nightingale* were this type of work, we might well hope that the discovery of a 'key' would help us make better sense of it. Since political writing offers a reason for concealment, there is some point to examining historical contexts – wishing, to be sure, that we were more certain of the poem's date.

There is another reason for feeling more hopeful about political allegory: a number of such works are cast as animal fables. I am aware of no vernacular examples as early as 1200, but they become quite frequent thereafter; *Renart le Bestornei*, for example, dates from the 1260s,[1] and according to U.T. Holmes 'It was the introduction of much serious [political] satire at the close of the thirteenth century which killed the appeal and consequently the popularity of these tales [stories about Renard].'[2] If *The Owl and the Nightingale* were indeed a thirteenth century poem, it might be part of this movement. Political allegory as a means of approaching the poem has been little explored until recently, but it deserves consideration. In the first part of this chapter, I shall examine the most detailed and impressive theory so far proposed; in the second and third, I shall deal with some other attempts more briefly, and consider generally the potentialities of this approach.

Anne W. Baldwin proposes that the altercation between Nightingale and Owl is related to the struggle between Henry II and Thomas Becket.[3] To aid understanding of her arguments, I should like to sketch those portions of the conflict which Baldwin considers relevant, italicizing details supposedly mentioned in the text.

> Upon becoming primate, Thomas Becket proved less tractable than Henry II had anticipated, so Henry drew up a list of the powers he intended to exercise over the Church – the Constitutions of Clarendon – and won the acquiescence of all the bishops but Becket, including *Gilbert Foliot*, Bishop of London and *Thomas's enemy*. Becket's continued resistance caused Henry to convene a kangaroo *court* at Northampton and try to humiliate Becket by bringing charges based on his deeds as chancellor. Henry *fined him preposterously large sums* for these alleged crimes. Becket refused to recognize the validity of the judgments passed on him. When it looked as if Henry would resort to violence in one of his blind rages – possibly murder, quite probably castration or other mutilation – Thomas fled Britain. He returned six years later, but immediately shattered the fragile truce by *excommunicating* those clergymen who had carried out various canonically illegal acts at Henry's behest during Thomas's *exile*. His *martyrdom* followed shortly afterwards (29 December 1170) as the result of just such a royal rage as that which he had fled in 1164. Henry was instantly in danger of *excommunication* and his land of interdict, but both disasters were averted. *Henry's peace with the Church* was finally cemented in 1174 when, having promised to give up all his uncanonical claims, he did a long open-air penance at Becket's tomb (*which brought on a severe fever*). To add to Henry's troubles that year, a horse kicked him on the shin and caused him to be *lame* for an appreciable time.

Baldwin's choice of historical context has much to recommend it. The Owl's asceticism, if not her gloom, is more or less appropriate to Thomas, and both the Owl and Thomas are martyred. Baldwin's interpretation accounts exceptionally well for that much discussed word 'foliot' (868): the Becket-Owl could well speak sourly of foolishness by punning on the name of his worst enemy, who spoke foolishness in the ear of the king and who is on record as having publicly called Thomas a 'fool.' Foliot, fool, folly, and foolishness blend very smoothly in this contemptuous exclamation. 'Ded ne lame' is also better utilized in this than in other interpretations. Kathryn Huganir's assertion that it was a 'current saying' seems flimsy when Baldwin can tie the phrase so exactly to King Henry's ailments of 1174.[4]

Another problem which Baldwin claims her approach surmounts is that of the comments on adultery. The Owl's sympathy for abandoned wives, even condoning retributive adultery, might echo thoughts of Becket, for Henry's infidelities were notorious. Moreover, Henry kept his wife in confinement for a decade (1173–83), rather like the jealous knight of line 1055. Baldwin explains another crux – 'mansing is so ibroded' (1312) – as alluding to the excommunications and threats of it rife just before and just after Becket's death. The 'Iesus his soule do merci!' she construes as consonant with the ecclesiastical view of Henry's soul just before and after the murder – near excommunicate and close to damned. Clearly the historical context Baldwin has chosen offers some really attractive parallels to the poem. However, fuller examination of her use of history reveals some major problems.

First, what is the relationship between the two birds and Henry and Becket? She states that 'the owl represents Thomas à Becket, Archbishop of Canterbury, and the Church's position' and implies that the Nightingale represents 'the position of Henry II and his court' (p. 207). Obviously there is a confusing imprecision in 'Becket ... and' or 'Henry II and.' Baldwin is denying a one-to-one correspondence of the sort usually found in political allegories; she is forced to do so because the Nightingale actually mentions Henry. But at no point does the Owl refer to Becket, and there is no reason to look on her as a supporter rather than the primate himself except the critic's desire for parallelism.

Henry's role in the poem is difficult to pin down. He appears in lines 1091–2: 'Þat underyat þe king Henri – / Iesus his soule do merci! – ' Baldwin admits that the pious wish is of the sort normally used for the dead, but cleverly argues, referring to contemporary clerical letters, that here it may be appropriate for the spiritual death of near-excommunication. Possibly so, but that interpretation makes the line implicitly critical of Henry. Would the royalist Nightingale have thought 'so gode kinges' soul in that much danger? Becket may have thought the king's soul lost, but many contemporaries considered Becket a power-crazy upstart whose opinion of Henry would have seemed anything but impartial or responsible. If Baldwin's historical explanation of the line is correct, it contradicts her interpretation of the Nightingale's character and hence her general reading.

Another passage which Baldwin tries to relate to historical conditions raises even more problems. This is the extended allusion to the jealous knight, his wife, and the Nightingale (1045–1110). Baldwin starts by equating the knight with Henry II – both put their wives under lock and key – and claims that the import of the anecdote is satirical, for Henry was far too guilty of adultery to cast the first stone. Leaving aside the objection that Eleanor's incarceration was partly for political reasons, we should notice that the lines telling how the knight locked his lady up – the only ones with any direct relevance to Henry – are put in the Nightingale's mouth, and she is outraged by the knight's behaviour. Would a supporter and alter ego of Henry's chide the knight and be sympathetic to the wife?

To make things more complex, Baldwin turns around and passes (without denying her first proposal) to the proposition that the knight is not Henry II but rather Thomas Becket, and his lady the English Church, who is being urged on to sin by a nightingale (Henry, or some royalist). She supports this identification with the evidence that even as 'king Henri' in the poem vastly overpunishes the knight, so too Henry II tried to impose impossibly great fines on Thomas for deeds which were minor crimes (if that) or for which Thomas had not been duly summoned and accused. Both Thomas and the knight went into exile as a result of such overpunishment. If all of these possibilities are kept in mind, then Henry Plantagenet appears (a) as good King Henry, (b) as the nightingale in the anecdote, (c) as the Nightingale of the poem (who is telling part of the anecdote), and (d) possibly as the jealous knight, though the knight may instead be Thomas Becket, Henry's enemy. I think some order can be found in this chaos but Baldwin harmed her thesis by positing this dual identification.

The attempt to equate the jealous knight with Henry seems most questionable, for with that identification, we find the pro-Thomas Owl

siding with the knight (Henry) and the pro-Henry Nightingale abusing
and criticizing this knight. Logically, a better case can be made for
Thomas as the knight, the Church as his wife. The Nightingale is then
a royalist who tries to tempt the Church to desert its rightful master.
King Henry punishes the knight excessively for rightfully protecting his
'wife,' and for trying to eliminate the tempter. Except for the problem
that it is the Nightingale who thinks the living Henry's soul to be in need
of mercy, the birds' attitudes make sense. But we know of no referent
for the nightingale-tempter, who would have to be a royalist whom
Thomas tried seriously to punish, either with the actual penalty for
treason (quartering by horses) or with spiritual punishment. (As Baldwin observes, the impenitent in Hell are jerked apart by four devils.)
Moreover, Thomas was not fined one hundred pounds, but over thirty
thousand pounds. And though Thomas lost his 'wunne' like the knight,
he could not and did not pay the king anything (unlike the knight, who
did pay) because without his lands he had no source of revenue, as Baldwin admits (p. 221).

Another problem is Baldwin's interpretation of Nicholas of Guildford. She tentatively identifies him with Nicholas, Archdeacon of London, a follower of Foliot and frequent messenger between him and King
Henry. She suggests that the poem is not a genuine plea for preferment,
but rather a satire on church corruption and an angry complaint that
benefices could be handed out to such a man. She claims that the poem
itself indicates Nicholas's undeservingness. The obscurity of his dwelling
she holds against him, for no one, even the Nightingale, would have been
ignorant of his home were he really famous for sound judicial decisions.
Another black mark is his plea for more than one benefice – unashamed
pluralism. And finally, Baldwin takes the statement (201–10) that he
once preferred nightingales, though would now choose owls, as proof
that in past times Nicholas was a false judge.

In reply, I think it can be said that obscurity of dwelling does not
prove anything about a man's qualifications. The pluralism charge looks
more damning to us from our modern perspective, but that is because
we are influenced by knowing which view of the subject won out. We
find it hard to believe that any moral person could be so brazen as
openly to demand extra livings, but we are equally uncomfortable with
the notion that Henry felt it his right to allow neither appeals to Rome
nor bishops to leave England without his permission, or, to quote Baldwin, that he 'refused to acknowledge [an] interdiction' on his continental

holdings for his part in Becket's murder. Henry's claims and practices were not unusual for the day. Only a few cranks versed in the newfangled canon law would have considered him seriously in the wrong. Though pluralism was disapproved by those concerned with ecclesiastical theory, it was to be decades before the rank and file would be made to look on it as reprehensible. Becket himself held a number of livings before he became chancellor – the churches of St Mary-le-Strand and Otford, and prebends at St Paul's and Lincoln, among others. Nicholas's desire for multiple livings looks suspicious to us, but we may be reading more into it than is warranted.

As for Nicholas's supposed change of views and previous false judgments, Baldwin's interpretation does not seem convincing. Judgments in this context are not black or white, good or bad, where no one but a consciously evil man could choose the bad; the two sides are merely royalist and ecclesiastical. In his days as chancellor, Becket himself prosecuted cases for Henry II and supported the 'royalist' side, even to the point of defying his old patron and friend Theobald, Archbishop of Canterbury. Yet at the time, such judgments presumably did not seem immoral to him. That Nicholas has changed his perspective does not necessarily mean his earlier judgments were consciously and deliberately fraudulent. And another drawback to Baldwin's handling of Nicholas of Guildford is her tentative identification of him. Would any pro-Thomas Owl willingly accept Nicholas, Archdeacon of London, as judge? Baldwin does not adduce any evidence that Archdeacon Nicholas changed sides. If he is really meant to stand for some sort of corruption within the Church, why are both Owl and Nightingale, and the Wren as well, so outspokenly laudatory? The Nightingale we could understand, but not the other two. Yet again, one of Baldwin's specific historical identifications clashes with her general interpretation.

Turning from some specific problems which show up in the course of Baldwin's arguments, I should like now to consider the more general drawbacks to this approach to the poem. One is the manner in which the poem is laid out: the closest bond between the Henry II-Becket struggle and the Nightingale-Owl conflict is the martyrdom of Becket and the Owl. In the poem we do not reach this parallel until the last two hundred lines. Baldwin asserts (p. 214) that 'If *The Owl and the Nightingale* was written shortly after 1174, the Suffering Servant [martyred Owl] obviously was Thomas Becket.' Without this parallel, however, the similarity between history and the text is rather slight, and we might well wonder if anyone would make the connection. If the auditor or reader is told that he will learn about King Noble the Lion and his vassal Renard, he can hastily assemble a mental list of kings and vassals likely to be commented on, and make the identification when details establish a clear correspondence. In *The Owl and the Nightingale*, we have no King Nightingale or Bishop Owl. Instead, we are given a great deal of real life avian detail which seems to establish these birds as birds rather than as historical figures. Baldwin's thesis would be helped considerably if a likeness to the Henry II-Becket quarrel emerged early in the poem, but what does come through is only the dichotomy of cheer and ascetic gloom, neither of which is appropriate to the temperaments of king or archbishop. Thomas was ascetic, but not notably gloomy, and Henry was more famous for his rages than for Franciscan-like joy. Baldwin stresses Henry's adultery as a link to the Nightingale, who is accused of celebrating carnal love and who admits to singing outside the windows of lords and ladies in bed. Singing of love and committing adultery are not equivalent. Moreover, love was not Henry's primary interest, but it does seem to be one of the Nightingale's. And when we look at her other interests – song, helping priests by cheering them, denouncing prophesying – we see little to relate her to the king. The pun on Foliot's name comes relatively early (868), but by itself is a rather slender clue, and the occasional references to King Henry as a figure existing outside the world of this bird quarrel tend to suggest that he is *not* represented by one of the birds. Is there a point in the poem at which a well-informed listener can feel absolutely sure that these identifications are correct? Even the Owl's martyrdom does not clinch the matter, for her death is patterned on Christ's, not Becket's. For the parallel to be incontrovertible, the Owl would have to be murdered at the behest of the Nightingale, preferably by four other birds. Even if more evidence appeared near the beginning of the poem, I doubt if we would ever feel the assurance in the identification that we do with *Absalom and Achitophel*.

Another major difference between poem and proposed context is the nature of the issues debated. If *The Owl and the Nightingale* were really an allegorical reflex of the Henry II-Becket quarrel, we would expect some similarity in the types of issues: at the very least, the birds should be claiming the right to determine each other's movements in various spheres of action. But nothing in the text appears to stand for such points of friction as punishment of criminous clerics or free ecclesiastical elections. The Nightingale does express willingness to take her case to Rome (745–6), but 'Ich graunti þat we go to dome / Tofore þe sulfe þe Pope of Rome' looks less like reference to a specific set of appeals than like an expression of confidence in her case. We get no sense of the Nightingale trying to strip the Owl of powers; the birds only try to prove each other useless and disliked by man, a very different sort of quarrel. The perspectives of men and birds are different: whereas Henry II and Becket quarrel over who is going to *rule* which portions of Christendom, the birds fight over which is better in an abstract sense, and which better *serves* mankind. This difference affects the spirit of each conflict.

In considering the Henry II-Becket interpretation, we must judge how well it covers all parts of the poem. The avian details have no special relevance, and the antagonism of the birds, built as it is largely on avian characteristics, does not fit the Church-State quarrel well. Points like the Owl's contempt for the Nightingale's refusal to go North fit the birds but not the historical figures. And who in the world of men is the Wren meant to represent? In bird lore, the wren is king, and may be functioning in that role as king among birds in *The Owl and the Nightingale*, for she does seem to be a figure of authority. But there is no historical figure – king, emperor, or pope – who functioned in the Henry II-Becket quarrel as she does. Baldwin's reading is plausible in its most general outline: vaguely churchly and secular figures quarrel, and the churchly one refers to its own martyrdom, but so many details contradict the identification that it seems to me untenable. At this point then we may ask whether other critics have been any more successful in trying to read *The Owl and the Nightingale* as historical allegory.

J.C. Russell, working from the same desire to find a historical key, decided upon a different decade, a new generation of figures, and a new Nicholas.[5] According to Russell, the poem's intended patron is Geoffrey, Archbishop-elect of York, the man needing a benefice Nicholas de Aquila (probably a canon lawyer at Oxford), the Owl and Nightingale respectively Geoffrey and his half-brother Richard I,[6] and the occasion of the poem a visit to Oxford by Geoffrey just after Christmas 1189. Like Baldwin, Russell traces general parallels between the life of an ecclesiast and the Owl, but has rather little evidence to back up the identification of the Nightingale. Like Baldwin also, he offers some interesting explanations of single line cruces, but these tend not to integrate well with the general interpretation.

Russell tackled the poem from the problem of recipient or patron. Geoffrey undoubtedly did patronize men of learning. On the grounds that a poem to Geoffrey might well include him among the protagonists, he notes that the Owl's position changes three times in the course of the poem, as Geoffrey's did throughout the year 1189. First Geoffrey, like the Owl, suffered an initial setback; he had been Henry II's mainstay while all Henry's legitimate sons ranged themselves in opposition; at Henry's death, he could hardly hope that Richard (the new king) would feel well disposed towards him. Then his position was secured by his being appointed Archbishop-elect of York, even as the Owl's position is by skilled rebuttal. Finally, the Owl is technically defeated and surrounded by little birds, and the outcome is left in doubt. Russell equates this with the concerted efforts of Geoffrey's enemies to prevent his consecration. The outcome of this effort was determined only after the papal legate confirmed the election on 14 December 1189, but the poet could not have known of this if he were writing his poem at that time for delivery immediately after Christmas.

Because Russell identifies the Owl as he does, the logical candidate for Nightingale is Richard. In support of this, however, he can only offer the details that Richard is known to have written songs and was associated with the warm south; further, the Nightingale is said to have an army of followers called the 'here' (1702, 1790), the mobile force a king could take anywhere, unlike the 'ferde' (mentioned in connection with the Owl [1684]) which is strictly for local defence.

Russell finds explanations for a number of short allusions. The singing in the North can represent England-based Geoffrey's antagonism towards Aquitaine-oriented Richard; and more specifically, Geoffrey went to Scotland early in 1189 on Richard's business. The Owl's lenient view of adultery is what one might expect from an illegitimate child of an adulterous relationship. Russell interprets the use of Alfredian proverbs and the reference to *good* King Henry as a sign that the patron felt flattered by reference to English royalty, and had felt more positive towards Henry than had his legitimate sons. Russell interprets the various issues raised in the debate as sops to diverse elements of an Oxford public audience: astrology for academics, married love for the bourgeois, cockfighting and gambling for parts of both town and gown, and discussion of such moral points as the deadly sins for theologians. And, of course, this interpretation does better than others at explaining the indeterminate jockeying between Nightingale and Owl, with no conclusion given; according to Russell's calculations, the author (who may, in his scheme of things, be distinct from Nicholas of Guildford) could not have known the outcome at the time he was writing the poem. Russell further suggests the intriguing idea that the piece may have been written as a bird poem in the first place on account of Nicholas de Aquila's name, since Aquila is both a family name and the Latin for 'eagle.'[7]

Perhaps the weakest point in this interpretation is the fact that in 1189 Richard and Geoffrey were not quarrelling in the sense that the Owl and Nightingale are sparring – they had done so in the past, but by late 1189, when Geoffrey accepted the archbishopric, their relative positions were settled. The Nightingale's technical victory and her triumphant gathering of little birds against the Owl do not fit the history. Russell equates the little birds with Geoffrey's enemies trying to prevent his consecration, but in the poem the Nightingale is definitely of the same party as the spiteful small birds. In history, Richard was promoting the consecration even more enthusiastically than Geoffrey himself, in hopes that once Geoffrey was made priest he could not make a bid for the throne.

A number of assumptions and arguments do not stand up well to careful scrutiny, the natures of the birds, for instance. Why should a bird supposedly representing Richard be so love-oriented? He was better known for crusading than for singing outside the bowers of lords and ladies. No explanation of the jealous knight anecdote (which figures the Nightingale) suggests itself in this context. Russell describes Geoffrey as 'virtuous, loyal and cantankerous,' but those characteristics have nothing to do with the crabbed asceticism of the Owl, and Geoffrey, despite his many years as bishop-elect of Lincoln, was anything but monkish. He had steadfastly refused to enter orders, hoping instead for secular advancement. Russell states (p. 179) that 'The pious line about Henry II and apparent reference to his faithful follower, Gilbert Foliot, indicate that association with English royalty flattered the patron.' But the pious reference to Henry and praise of him as a good king (1091–5) are uttered by the Nightingale-Richard, who proved himself lacking in respect and love for Henry. Furthermore, the allusion to Foliot incontrovertibly puns on the word with the meaning of folly or foolishness; Henry's faithful follower is not being praised, he is being ridiculed by the Owl-

Geoffrey, so neither reference offers much flattery to the patron as Russell conceives him. Nor does the name de Aquila seem relevant, since no eagle appears and Nicholas is never called by this family name. And finally, there are drawbacks to Russell's hypothesis that various subjects are touched on to please various portions of the audience. This may in part be true, but surely it is stretching a point to imply that rowdies would feel the poem more worth listening to because there are one line allusions to gaming and to the cock's ability to fight (1666, 1679). And would 'the eulogy of married love and of the devoted wife' (p. 184) really please a lay audience any more than a witty anti-feminist diatribe? Would references to married love really make any women in the audience feel better disposed toward the poem than they otherwise would have felt? Granting that medieval poets were not sensitive to what we think of as organic unity, these seem less satisfactory reasons for the poet's references to such subjects than we would like. In sum, I think Russell's attempt to find a historical context interesting, and quite original in his concern with the patron, but ultimately no more satisfactory than Baldwin's. In neither case do details, general interpretation, and possible rationale for the poem's form and composition so fit together that we come away with a firm sense that we know what the poem is.

Why have these attempts to read it as political allegory failed? Is it just that the right context has not yet been recognized, or are there more fundamental problems? The idea seems at least superficially plausible. After all, we do have political allegories cast in animal terms from a period not much later than the dates these critics have in mind.

I would like to suggest that it is this very animal form which is misleading to critics who seek historical contexts. Because animals are protagonists, we feel justified in trying political allegory, yet we might not do that so hastily if we considered the nature of the conflict. This poem has virtually no plot at all. Political allegories, though, are usually worked up as animal fables or stories. Characteristic of the fable is the straightforward tale and a clear, blunt moral which is meant to be relevant not just to King Noble and Renard, for instance, but to the human king and vassal who are analogous, and even to the general reader. Viewed in these terms, *The Owl and the Nightingale* suddenly looks rather less like the usual historical allegory. It has no story and no moral: even if a historical figure were to recognize himself in one of the birds, what would he learn? Their conflict is so indeterminate it tells us nothing. From the

Nun's Priest's Tale, we can deduce basic lessons about pride, but even if we were to try, we would have trouble extracting any such tidy moral from *The Owl and the Nightingale*.

What then are we to make of the historical references in *The Owl and the Nightingale*? There do seem to be some allusions to historical events and personages – King Henry and (probably) Gilbert Foliot, a ruler neither 'ded ne lame,' a curious grouping of northern countries visited by a man from Rome – taken together, these look as if they ought to add up to something, but no satisfactory answer has emerged. With political allegory as with intellectual, correspondences between portions of the poem and extrinsic contexts are not hard to find, but one such partial congruence does not make the whole poem a vehicle for commentary on the subject unless much firmer proofs can be offered than already have been. Critical sanity demands that the whole poem be taken into account.

Another attempt to interpret the poem by tying it to a specific historical context deserves mention. A.C. Cawley (*MLR* 1951), working with the passage on prophecy (1145–1330), concludes that the poem was written in connection with a conjunction of Saturn and Mars in Libra in 1186, and that the two birds may be viewed as roughly saturnian and venerian, as well as pro- and anti-astrology. He demonstrates that the misfortunes which the Owl predicts belong to the purview of Saturn and Mars, backing up his analysis with quotations from astrological treatises and with pleasingly apt lines from the *Knight's Tale*. Mars and Saturn are in conjunction in Libra approximately every thirty years, however, so we have no reason to consider 1186 a more likely date than the conjunctions of thirty or sixty years later, if Ker's redating of the C text is accepted. Also troublesome to this interpretation is the fact that *most* misfortunes, except those associated with love, are sponsored by these two malign planets, so any list of disasters may accidentally appear to have astrological significance.

The plausibility of Cawley's reading depends heavily upon the chroniclers' report that everybody knew of the conjunction and feared the disasters which were expected to attend it.[8] Though these assertions obviously cannot be disproved, they must be questioned. Had astrologers really been concerned, we would expect more agreement on the nature of the event in the heavens. Roger of Hoveden's sources speak variously of a conjunction of all the planets, or of Mars and Saturn, while one of them, Pharamella of Cordova, actually *denies* that Mars and Saturn would indeed be in conjunction on the appointed day. Pharamella goes on to point out that if Mars and Saturn in Libra cause disasters, then such must occur at thirty year intervals, which, he points out, we know not to be the case. Roger of Hoveden's own approach to his material is worth noting. He cites his saracen and English authorities with great relish and in full detail under the year 1184 when writings on the event first appeared; his enthusiasm is that of a newsman delighted at being able to report so colourful an item as Corumphiza's gloomy forecast. Though he is always interested in climatic events, and reports several during 1185, he never mentions the conjunction and any disasters or lack thereof in 1186, when they were 'expected' to occur. Had the anticipatory panic he reports been widespread, we would expect reference to it, or to the relief following the passing of the fatal day. If we put these objections aside, we must still solve the problem of the function of all the non-astrological portions of the poem, and ask what we are meant to conclude about astrology from the debate. There is no intrinsic reason to discard Cawley's date of 1186 or shortly thereafter as impossible, but neither does it seem any sounder than 1174–5 (Baldwin), 1182–3 (Huganir), December 1189 (Russell), or 1194–5 (Tupper), all of whom work from 'internal evidence.'

We can learn something about the problems of treating *The Owl and the Nightingale* as a political or historical allegory if we look at various famous clashes of the twelfth and thirteenth centuries and see what they can tell us about *The Owl and the Nightingale* by contrast. The contestants who suggest themselves are the Popes and Emperors (or other lesser representatives of Church and State[9]) Henry II and Louis VII, Eleanor of Aquitaine and Louis VII, and Abelard and Bernard. Others would be possible – John and Stephen Langton or Henry III and Simon de Mountfort – but the four I have chosen cover a reasonable spread of types of conflict, and the last two would only be repetitions of the basic patterns present in these four or in Baldwin's and Russell's studies.

When we consider the struggles between empire and papacy, we would presumably link any chosen pope with the Owl because of her religiosity, and the appropriate emperor, willy-nilly, would be cast as Nightingale. But objections immediately spring to mind. There is nothing that would lead us to think of the Holy Roman Empire as the milieu, or of those men as the actors. The number of allusions to England and the North, and to English personages would tend to direct attention to those parts, even if we can only say that they indicate the author's milieu, not that of the allegory. But if the allegory were supposed to concern distant figures, we might expect a hint of local colour to orient us.

If we consider Louis VII's relations with Eleanor of Aquitaine (marital) or Henry II (martial), we find that a case could be made for either set of identifications. Louis was monkish and ascetic, and might seem a good referent for the Owl. Eleanor, the dashing young heiress of Aquitaine, might well have seemed like the Nightingale to some – partial to the south, and so scandalously concerned with love that, on a crusade to the Holy Lands, she was believed to be carrying on an affair with her own uncle. The Wren might be cast as Bernard of Clairvaux, who helped Louis annul the marriage. If one prefers to view the Nightingale as Henry II, the quarrel might in some way reflect the skirmishing warfare waged almost continuously between him and Louis. Perhaps the rally of small birds in support of the Nightingale about the Owl, with no definitive result, might be meant as a representation of the time Henry and his army had Louis bottled up in Toulouse (1159), but refused to take the city by storm because he did not wish to attack his feudal overlord directly, though Thomas Becket strenuously urged it. But anyone wishing to demolish these identifications can do so easily enough. The lack of plot seems ill-designed to reflect either quarrel, even if small portions of the text may seem to offer parallels to the historical situations.

The clash between Abelard and Bernard, although it suffers from most of these same drawbacks, is a more tempting analogy because it seems to agree even in minor details with the general antinomy of character. The Owl is monastic, probably white (i.e., Cistercian), austere, and very indignant at the Nightingale's powers of pleasing and seducing her auditors. The Nightingale, like Abelard, is highly welcome to most who hear her, but according to some (like the Owl and Bernard), her song is dangerous. Bernard thought Abelard's teachings dangerous intellectually and spiritually, for their point was not the urging of men to weep for their sins. Many of the charges linking the Nightingale's song to sin can be read allegorically in this light, but some can also be taken quite literally, for Abelard's affair with Heloise and its consequences were notorious. At the time of the affair, Abelard tells us, he wrote love songs which became immensely popular. Some of the Owl's gibes about the Nightingale's lust and interest in carnal matters might be construed as referring to Abelard's private life. The jealous knight who tried to prevent his lady from doing 'An vnriȝt of hire licome' (1054), and who inflicted an excessive punishment on the Nightingale resembles Canon Fulbert. The Nightingale's comment that a man who commits adultery may 'for-leose þat þer hongeþ' (1485) seems tantalizingly allusive to Abelard's castration, though, of course, Abelard was not actually committing adultery, and the canon was no wronged husband. Furthermore, we know that the conflict between Abelard and Bernard was followed with interest by churchmen in England. Walter Map sketches a vivid little scene in which Thomas Becket and two Cistercian abbots discuss a letter written by Bernard to Pope Eugenius ranting against Abelard; Abelard had the sympathy of at least some of those present, for Map adds a scurrilous anecdote about Bernard immediately afterward. Map also describes the two Cistercians passing their news on to Gilbert Foliot.[10] But, of course, the same objections apply here as elsewhere: the issues debated, the avian details, the astrology, and the actual stands on adultery remain unaccounted for. The house of cards climbs skyward promisingly – but collapses. It is easy to propose new contexts, and with the new dating of the C text some thirteenth century contexts are bound to be tried, but ultimately such endeavours are likely to be fruitless.

Before haring off after more contextual keys, we might pause to consider a basic question. What would the poem have to be like to make political or historical allegory more promising as a critical approach? First, we might expect some sort of *story* concerning the birds, unless the historical figures were actually famed for a debate. Whether they were known for debate or more active antagonism, we might expect the issues the birds quarrel over to bear some resemblance to those which engaged the human antagonists; the sources of friction might be couched in avian terms, but their relations to human concerns should be clear. Thus if the men were monarchs fighting over territory, we would expect territorial or jurisdictional claims to appear in the birds' arguments – disagreement over who had the right to gather bugs between the old oak and the river. An allegorical interpretation based on a historical clash would seem more plausible if the Nightingale's objections to the Owl were not to her looks, gloom, tolerance towards the north and winter and darkness, and later to the Owl's ability to prophesy.

The use of thinly disguised human institutions would also make a political interpretation more likely. In the stories about Renard, there is a *King* Noble, who has a castle, a feudal court, vassals, and the like.

Such details of setting are very useful at the beginning of a tale if the audience is to recognize in the beasts the appropriate human analogues. In short, these would give us an appropriate general context to relate the story to, and such a clear-cut context for *The Owl and the Nightingale* is utterly lacking.

The great advantage to political allegory is the devastating clarity with which it can expose the folly or criminality of some public figure or faction. *The Owl and the Nightingale* lacks a readily ascertainable moral lesson, unless we are meant to conclude only that arguments between pig-headed opponents are not likely to reach productive conclusions; and even that does not really seem to be the moral, for the outcome is not utter stalemate – the birds agree to accept arbitration. This lack of message or commentary should weigh very heavily against political allegory as the key to *The Owl and the Nightingale*. Marvelous as it would be to find a historical context that would turn this baffling poem into a simple *à clef* matter, we ought to recognize that the poem lacks the usual earmarks of political allegory. It is cast in animal terms, but it does not have a clear context, a story with a definite outcome, or anything like the usual sort of moral. Yet these missing features are crucial to effective political allegory, and that being the case, we should realize how unlikely it is that *The Owl and the Nightingale* was written with that form in mind.

NOTES

1 See Edward Billings Ham, *Rutebeuf and Louis IX*, University of North Carolina Studies in the Romance Languages and Literatures 42 (Chapel Hill: University of North Carolina Press 1962), a discussion and edition of *Renart le Bestornei*.
2 *A History of Old French Literature* (1936; rev. ed. New York: Russell and Russell 1962) 211
3 'Henry II and *The Owl and the Nightingale*' *JEGP* 66 (1967) 207–29
4 Huganir, p. 92. Tupper, p. 416, paraphrases the expression 'dead or infirm' (i.e., feeble, sick), which seems adequate but less exact than Baldwin's explanation.
5 'The Patrons of *The Owl and the Nightingale*' *PQ* 48 (1969) 178–85
6 He adds the reservation (p. 181) that he does not wish to identify the men too closely with the birds. In effect, this frees him (without justification) from having to explain any details which do not quite fit his theory.
7 The seat of the de Aquila family, as he points out, is seven miles from Guildford, Surrey. Hence the alleged by-form 'of Guildford.'

8 See Benedict of Peterborough's *Gesta Regis Henrici Secundi*, ed. William Stubbs, Rolls Series 49, I 324 ff., and Roger of Hoveden's *Chronica*, ed. William Stubbs, Rolls Series 51, II 290 ff.

9 Margaret Schlauch, in *English Medieval Literature and its Social Foundations* (Warsaw: Państwowe Wydawnictwo Naukowe 1956) 161, argues for a variant of church *vs* state: she identifies the Owl with the clergy in general, and the Nightingale with the nobility. As usual, this approach works in part, but not completely. The Nightingale's claims to religious worth, the material on prophecy, avian details, and the like do not fit the interpretation.

10 See Walter Map, *De Nugis Curialium*, ed. Montague Rhodes James, Anecdota Oxoniensia, mediaeval and modern series, part xiv (Oxford: Clarendon Press 1914) 38-9.

6

structure and sequential impact

In the last four chapters, I have made a systematic attempt to assess the potentialities of the usual critical approaches to the poem. As we have seen, many critics implicitly consider the poem incomplete as it stands. They see in it no meaning or *raison d'être*, and so have felt compelled to seek external contexts which can supply an appropriate message. Bird lore, generic form, and various sorts of allegorical referents have been tried, but the results are certainly discouraging. Not only are the readings radically contradictory, but the extrinsic critical approaches have so far proved incapable of encompassing the entire poem – and the problem seems to lie in the methodology, not in the powers of the critics who have reached such frustratingly diverse conclusions. The avian detail, the dizzying twists and turns of the argument, and the peculiar patchwork of ideas comprised by the poem have proved disconcertingly resistant to tidy *à clef* explanations.

If the importation of extrinsic meanings is fundamentally unsound, then we have no choice but to return to the text. Nor is that a counsel of despair; much of its potential is untapped. Critics have become accustomed to looking through the poem for details to support their hypotheses, and have paid no attention to the way in which the reader's reactions should change as the poem progresses. Yet it seems to me that different parts are designed to elicit very different responses, and that this manipulation of audience reaction is one of the poem's most important features. Critics have been too ready to make statements about the proper response to the poem 'as a whole,' while ignoring the rather disparate nature of its parts. An equally promising subject for consideration is the structure of the poem. Though it has long been ignored, I believe that there is a quite clear structure, that it gives the work its forward movement and explains the arrangement of the birds' arguments, and that this organization is well-calculated to govern the reader's response. By returning to the text and reading it with attention to sequential impact and structure, I think we can proceed towards understanding the nature of the poem.

The first narrative unit (1–214), in terms of both structure and development of argument, is delimited by the birds themselves: once they recognize the fruitlessness of screaming at each other, they agree to change tactics and debate formally before a judge. Within this movement of the altercation, we receive all our first impressions; such feelings are notoriously difficult to change, and will influence our response to the whole work unless the poet takes very considerable steps to make us change our views.

The first impression is that this will be a lawsuit ('plait,' 5) between two birds, and I think that almost anybody, in any century, confronted with such a subject, would start by assuming that the birds are intended to bear some relation to man, possibly as mere mouthpieces for human concerns, possibly as satirically distorting mimics, possibly (though this would be unusual and surprising) as admirable models of virtue for man to respect and emulate. The audience naturally tries to fathom the nature of the connection: could it be that the birds represent specific celebrities? general philosophies? or just any member of the human race in some sort of quarrel situation? Listeners are likely to wonder fleetingly whether the birds are prominent political figures, or whether law court procedures are being satirized. The impression that the birds are in some fashion comparable to man is reinforced as we go on. Their songs are likened to man's instrumental music, they can talk, and when they do, they even take on a few of man's physical characteristics: the Nightingale says she would rather spit than sing (39) – birds cannot spit, but men do. That the relationship is satiric rather than didactically exemplary is confirmed when we see the birds being made fun of, not being held up for admiration. And since we are given no hints suggesting political allegory – no Bishop Brimstone the Owl – we are left undecided about how to think of them, but do quickly see that what they imply about mankind is far from complimentary. If one were to choose a single word to characterize the impression given by this section, it would be 'triviality.' The arguments are the silliest, the least substantial of any in the poem, the birds behave with crude nastiness, and our emotional engagement with them is correspondingly slight. As I have said once before, they sound like children from differing cultural or religious backgrounds; though ignorant of the real meaning of their traditional enmity, they chant trite insults and each would gladly hurt the other should an opportunity arise.

Consider the grievance aired in this section, and the tone. The Nightingale's speech is typical:

Ich wot þat þu art unmilde
VViþ hom þat ne muȝe from þe schilde,
& þu tukest vvroþe & vuele,
VVhar þu miȝt, over smale fuȝele.
Vorþi þu art loþ al fuelkunne,
& alle ho þe driueþ honne,
& þe bischricheþ & bigredet
& vvel narewe þe biledet;
& ek forþe þe sulue mose
Hire þonkes wolde þe totose.
Þu art lodlich to biholde,
& þu art loþ in monie volde:
Þi bodi is short, þi swore is smal,
Grettere is þin heued þan þu al;
Þin eȝene boþ colblake, & brode
Riȝt svvo ho weren ipeint mid wode.
Þu starest so þu wille abiten
Al þat þu mist mid cliure smiten.
Þi bile is stif & scharp & hoked
Riȝt so an ovvel þat is croked.
Þarmid þu clackes oft & longe,
& þat is on of þine songe.
Ac þu þretest to mine fleshe,
Mid þine cliures woldest me meshe:
Þe were icundur to one frogge,
[Þat sit at mulne vnder cogge:]
Snailes, mus & fule wiȝte

Boþ þine cunde & þine riȝte.
Þu sittest a dai & fliȝ[s]t a niȝt.
Þu cuþest þat þu art on vnwiȝt.
Þu art lodlich & unclene –
Bi þine neste ich hit mene,
& ek bi þine fule brode:
Þu fedest on hom a vvel ful fode.
Vel wostu þat hi doþ þarinne:
Hi fuleþ hit up to þe chinne ...

(61–96)

Notice that the issues are behaviour, popularity, looks, diet, and toilet habits, all trivial bases for estimating somebody's character. Of course, human religious or racial prejudices are fuelled by just such minor differences. In human contexts, we may be too blinded to see the idiocy of judging on such grounds, but in avian terms, the insignificance of the grievances is clear. We might well feel disgust at the birds' streak of cruelty were it not that they are just birds, and that the excited zest with which they sling their insults robs them of most of the bitterness which characterizes most such human exchanges.

The Owl groans at her inability to engage her opponent in physical combat. Despite the real provocation, her frustration wins her little sympathy, for she has as much advantage in size and weapons as a man with a knife fighting a child. The Nightingale naturally refuses to venture into the lists (153–70); being the weaker, she prefers lawsuit to judicial combat and proposes a verbal match (181–6), which she obviously expects to win. The Owl, for lack of alternative, agrees.

Clearly these exchanges are pointless. All the differences are natural, indeed God-given. The characteristics of neither bird impinge on the prerogatives of the other: the Nightingale may be put off her song by the Owl's proximity, but if so, it is her own fault. Neither the sight nor sound of the Owl ought to make any difference to her. It is not as if owls regularly prey upon nightingales or automatically attack them. She presumably would have been perfectly safe had she not started the quarrel with her insults. There is no justification for the fight; no principle is at stake, no beliefs are challenged or threatened. The birds fight over physical differences which they cannot control – habits of eating, flying, and singing – not moral disagreements. Yet each would be glad to kill the other if given a chance.

Not only do we see the silliness of the issues, but we recognize the ugliness of the outlook behind such bickering. What could be more repulsive than the Owl's ghoulish regrets over her inability to get at the Nightingale and strangle her? Nor are the Nightingale's jeers much better. The petty nastiness appears at the very beginning when 'aiþer aȝen oþer sval / & let þat vvole mod ut al' (7–8). It continues to manifest itself physically, as when the Owl swells (145–6), and mentally in the gratuitous cruelty of the Nightingale's story about a baby owl in a falcon's nest (101–38). Such a fight excites disgust, but our dominant response is amusement, because it seems too silly to be taken seriously.

Nor is the shallowness of our response solely the result of the nature of the altercation. We might tend to take such a squabble seriously on the subconscious assumption that birds who talk are *ipso facto* thinly disguised men, had not the author manoeuvred us into viewing the birds from an objective distance by providing the poem with a human narrator. At the beginning of the poem, we are quite aware that we are receiving all our impressions through this intermediary: '*Ich* was in one sumere dale ... Iherde *ich* holde grete tale' and the like. We do not plunge headlong into the issues and forget the protagonists; the narrator feeds us descriptive avian detail and sets the scene so that we are forced to look down on the squabblers. Though we lose awareness of the narrator once we get involved in the exchanges, he is responsible for our strong initial impression that the contestants are only birds engaged in a silly fight, not debaters deserving serious concern. So firmly are they established as birds, in fact, that we may very early begin to think that they are meant to be comparable to men in only a very general sense. They appear to be connected to men somehow, as we are reminded from time to time by clusters of human terms applied to their quarrel – legal jargon and musical terms for example – but the birds certainly do not look like disguised celebrities as the poem wears on.

The narrator not only creates this distance between audience and protagonists, he helps make the distance satiric. His introducing the birds with the mock seriousness of law court diction encourages us to view them as 'low' figures who ironically diminish the solemn business involved in man's quarrelling. He draws attention to the altercation's ugliness with such graphic details as 'aiþer aȝen oþer sval.' As the poem advances and our sense of there being an intermediary disappears, we become more caught up in the quarrel. At the beginning, however, we are encouraged in every way to stand far enough back to see the trivial nature of the quarrel, but not so far that we reject the whole piece as beneath consideration. We can accept it as ugly and silly, but entertaining, because of the incongruities introduced by the avian nature of the protagonists. The narrator guides us from the world of men to that of birds in such a way that we listen for fun to this fight between screeching balls of feathers, and we do not need to impose on them such weighty concerns that they can no longer amuse us by their likeness to men.

The second major narrative block (214–548) corresponds to the beginning of a formal lawsuit, and consists of the Nightingale's attack, a partial rebuttal, and a more elaborate attack. This section comes to a natural, formal conclusion when the Owl invokes court procedural rules, even as the initial narrative unit ended with the formal decision to debate. This second passage differs from the first mainly in that the arguments no longer dwell exclusively on physical avian trivialities. The Nightingale introduces moral overtones into her accusations and we begin to hear more echoes of human quarrels. Thus, where before she merely scorned the Owl's song, she now tries to discredit it for what she considers its unnecessarily mournful quality (219–26). Further, the Nightingale reuses an epithet she tossed out casually earlier (33, 90), and tries to exploit its full force to disqualify the Owl entirely as an 'unwiȝt,' a monster outside the natural order of the universe, because she is active at night, the time for evil (217–53). This would be a decisive charge if it could be sustained, but, of course, it cannot. Indeed, the Nightingale (night-singer) herself is as vulnerable to it as her opponent. This struggle at first seems more justifiable than the fight concerning looks, because in a Christian world, everyone is supposed to try to vanquish evil: were the Owl an 'unwiȝt,' the Nightingale's belligerence would be laudable. Her inability to establish her point, however, and her own habit of functioning nocturnally, make her whole accusation look trumped up and, because we see through it, both amusing and contemptible.

As we move on, the Nightingale broadens her base of attack and adds yet more moral weight to it by accusing the Owl not just of singing unduly mournfully but of enjoying men's sorrow; she likens the Owl to one who 'wolde þat he iseȝe / Teres in evrich monnes eȝe' (425–6). This accusation, again based on a point of ethics, does not stand up any better than the first. The Owl is able to play the same game, and her claim that the Nightingale sings of lust (498) has the same sort of moral flavour. Throughout all these exchanges, the original audience presumably riffled through its mental file-cards to find a corresponding human quarrel, but, I rather imagine, with inconclusive results; though the terms of the birds' arguments are suggestive of any number of human disputes, the correspondences are not exact, and purely avian detail keeps intruding. Moreover, though the quarrel becomes more weighty, it is not more worthy of serious consideration. Had the author kept the fight on the trivial physical grounds of the first movement, we would rapidly have grown bored with such inconsequence. To the extent that we see the quarrel as an indictment of man's fights, we would feel that it was losing its relevance, for, we would tell ourselves, men's quarrels have more at stake. So the import is made to seem deeper, but at the same time, it is kept from becoming too serious by the introduction of logical flaws. The Owl, for instance, has been attacked for the 'grisliness' of her song (224). She defends it illogically, saying it sounds like a great horn whereas the Nightingale's sounds like a shrill pipe (318–19). But no evidence is proffered that horn is preferable to pipe, and the listeners know perfectly well that they would far rather hear the Nightingale, whatever instrument she may be like. Or again, the Nightingale says the Owl sings mournfully in winter, but the Owl claims she is joining in men's festivities and helping men celebrate Christmas by chanting *conduts*. Yet the audience is aware that such Owl-hoots would if anything cast a pall over the festivities by portending bad luck or disaster. Just as telling is the flaw in the Nightingale's logic when she prides herself on cheering and entertaining men, but refuses to perform during the winter when men need cheering most. After all, men would be cheerful in the summer without her aid; her song would be far more helpful when darkness and cold oppress men. The author does not exploit these contradictions to the full. His restraint, however, treats the listeners to the pleasure of seeing through the birds' manoeuvring on their own. The transparent flaws in the birds' logic help us maintain our superior, detached perspective, even if we feel more concern for them, and it helps preserve the 'lowness' which lets the birds parallel man satirically rather than seriously. Their lack of logic has usually been slighted by critics, but seems to me of paramount importance to interpreting the poem soundly.

The third narrative unit (549–1652) develops out of the second, just as the second evolved from the first. Basically the moral import of some of the accusations deepens, this time to the point that the birds have to defend themselves quasi-theologically. Yet the lightness of the poem is maintained by means of yet more flagrant illogic and by the highlighting of avian detail. And both illogic and avian detail keep us from identifying the quarrel with any one human dispute.

The transition again corresponds to law court procedure; the Owl goes from the defensive to the offensive, so she is the one who formulates the initial attack now, not the Nightingale. Amusingly, she starts, as did the Nightingale, with purely physical, trivial avian charges, and she utters them in the same nasty way the Nightingale did:

Þu nart bute on forworþe þing:
On þe nis bute chatering.
Þu art dim an of fule howe,
An þinchest a lutel soti clowe.
Þu nart fair, no þu nart strong,
Ne þu nart þicke, ne þu nart long.
Þu hauest imist al of fairhede,
An lutel is al þi godede.
An oþer þing of þe ich mene:
Þu nart vair, ne þu nart clene
Wane þu comest to manne haʒe,
Þar þornes boþ & ris idraʒe
Bi hegge & bi þicke wode.
Þar men goþ oft to hore node
Þarto þu draʒst, þarto þu wnest,
An oþer clene stede þu schunest.
Wan ich flo niʒtes after muse
I mai þe uinde ate rumhuse;
Among þe wode, among þe netle
Þu sittest & singst bihinde þe setle.
Þar me mai þe ilomest finde
Þar men worpeþ hore bihinde.
ʒet þu atuitest me mine mete
An seist þat ich fule wiʒtes ete;

Ac wat etestu – þat þu ne liȝe! –
Bute attercoppe & fule uliȝe
& wormes, ȝif þu miȝte finde
Among þe uolde of harde rinde?

(575–602)

The passage is just a list of insults on diet, looks, and habitat – all natural characteristics. Clearly the author is reminding us once again, just as
we enter a more serious phase, that the protagonists are merely birds,
not mouthpieces for men. Furthermore, this regression in argumentative
level serves to show that the Owl is intrinsically no more worthy than
the Nightingale, a necessary demonstration, for throughout the debate
she cultivates a holier-than-thou stance. The triviality and comic disgust-
ingness of the charges briefly reintroduces the humour of the earliest part
of the poem, helpful in maintaining a light tone where the arguments give
the appearance of getting more serious. Humour also sparkles in the Owl's
proud claims of helping man by cleansing churches of mice (609–10) –
an action that is hardly as altruistic as the Owl would have us believe,
since she does it for food.

The Nightingale seems to feel greatly set back by the Owl's charges,
but finally decides with grand illogic that if 'bale is alre hecst,' then 'bote
[must be] alre nest.' She is so sure of her defence that she would be willing to submit it to the Pope himself, it being a quasi-theological justification of her song. She does her best to link her singing with the eternal
verities of Christianity, though to do so she has to embrace a relatively
new – or, as the Owl would say, radical and subversive – religious attitude. The author adds the very pleasing touch of letting her claim that
she helps clerics (729–42) parallel the Owl's very similar claim (323–30),
just as the Owl's offensive, based on natural differences, parallels the
Nightingale's original charges. The similarities are so marked that as we
hear the second occurrences, we should remember the earlier examples
and recognize with amusement that in some ways the birds are very
similar, however much they might dispute that observation.

The Nightingale goes on to assert the superiority of her wit to the
Owl's strength, and then of her one talent over the Owl's many. She is
impressed by the Owl's claims to multiple talents, even if *we* can see the
extent to which they are satirically undercut by their dishonesty or illo-

gic – the Owl's claim to 'clean' churches, for instance, or her claim to comfort men in winter when she is really scaring them. In the Nightingale's attempt to prove her one virtue greater than any number the Owl can muster, she cites the fable of the cat and the fox (805–36), even as earlier she attacked the Owl by means of the fable of the falcon's nest. In a stunningly garbled argument, she tries to prove that one trick that works is better than any number that do not, but fails to establish the fact that her one works, that it has moral worth – and it is the moral worth which is under attack. Moreover, when listing the fox's 'uele wrenche,' she mentions tree climbing – 'he kan hongi bi þe boȝe' (816) – the one trick which supposedly makes the cat superior!

It cannot be said that the Owl notices these flaws: she is too feather-brained herself to know illogic when she sees it, and so just keeps hammering at the Nightingale's general worthlessness, using the same sorts of arguments that old-fashioned monks used against proponents of 'new' religion. The Owl is really no more logical than the Nightingale: the assertion in lines 877–8 is utterly destructive of the serious effect of her argument: 'Ȝif riȝt goþ forþ, & abak wrong, / Betere is mi wop þane þi song.' Although her telling points have the air of being lucky hits rather than cunning strokes, she does rather well when she accuses the Nightingale of celebrating lust, and discredits her for not singing in the North. The Nightingale loses further sympathy when she unburdens herself of her prejudiced assessment of Northerners (997–1014), for it is based on precisely those details of diet, habit, and habitat whose silliness we recognize when the insults are avian.

The Owl's move to charge the Nightingale with causing men to sin (and hence to go to hell) is the most serious accusation she has yet levelled (894–900). It marks a new step in the progression of the argument and leads to one of the two partly serious passages in the poem, here the description of the punishment of a nightingale for supposedly inciting a woman to commit adultery (1045–1110). This passage, like that on the Owl's crucifixion, is peculiar in that the Nightingale seems to describe her own death as if it had already taken place. While this incongruity can be explained away, the peculiarity of this perspective makes us uncomfortably aware of the unpleasant, even fatal, results of clashes (this time between man and bird). But lest the poem become too heavy and lose its satiric perspective, we are treated to the picture of the Nightingale boasting exultantly of a wergeld so excessive (£100) that the sum looks somehow fictitious, and certainly incongruous enough to warrant a laugh.

The last eight hundred lines of the poem are concerned directly or indirectly with the birds' deaths. The Nightingale runs afoul of angry husbands because of her association with adultery. She discusses her intentions at length in the latter part of the poem, but does not manage to exculpate herself completely. Her shocked incomprehension of how anybody could commit adultery yields a great deal of fun at her expense. Desdemona fails to be totally convincing in a similar asseveration, yet we have reason for taking her seriously. When this feather-duster solemnly assures us that there is absolutely nothing in adultery that could possibly give pleasure, we laugh. The birds' long discussion of adultery, which has little relevance to most interpretations, may best be accounted for by the fact that adultery is responsible for the Nightingale's death. And the Owl's stand on the lapses of wives, though not altogether in character, may be meant to remind us of how similar the birds really are, for the Nightingale similarly defends the lapses of maidens.

The other subject they explore at length in the last eight hundred lines is prophecy, the Owl's bane. The Owl is killed by man not because her song is mournful, but because men resent her supposed ability to predict calamities, and feel irrationally that she herself *causes* the disasters. The Nightingale rides the issue of prophecy for what it is worth; she feels sure that somehow she can use it to discredit the Owl because it causes men to attack her. The Owl has good answers, however, so the Nightingale has to keep shifting her ground. Thus she first speaks of the Owl's tendency to harp on unpleasant subjects as if it were merely a nasty habit which the Owl ought, in good taste, to forego, but the Owl points out that her warnings can be of great assistance to men. Were men to act on her warnings, they might often avoid the impending trouble altogether. Or so she says, and the Nightingale is impressed. But we know that the Owl's hooting is less informative than she thinks; hearing it would not tell us whether our houses were about to burn or a plague to descend. Our human perspective lets us see certain amusing lapses in the Owl's logic, but the birds themselves obviously both believe in their ability to communicate. The Owl also deserves another laugh as she self-importantly lauds herself for 'book learning' (1207–8) which she presumably does not really possess. Her boast that she knows ever so much (which she cannot be bothered to tell the Nightingale) about the Gospel (1209-10) has been taken as an allusion to the learned pretensions of some religious group, but it may well signify nothing more than the Owl's desire to capitalize on her reputation for wisdom in order to overawe her opponent.

The Owl's claim that her warnings should help men is a point with which she might have hoped to win the debate, for the Nightingale's claims to helpfulness have not been very successful. The Nightingale, however, stumbles on the tactic of trying to discredit the Owl's ends by discrediting her means. She raises the dread charge of witchcraft (1300-1), an accusation comparable in seriousness to her earlier attempt to prove the Owl an 'unwi3t' which, if substantiated, would not only defeat the Owl but justify her being killed. To the detriment of her cause, the Nightingale does not have the sense to stop and demand rebuttal; instead, she blunders on, raising the question of whether the Owl learns the future from the stars, and then denying the possibility. Consequently, the Owl never has to answer the witchcraft charge. She pounces on the Nightingale's alleged connection with love (which the Nightingale admits) and deflects the attack to the Nightingale, though the Owl too undercuts her own strong position by condoning the adultery of vengeful wives. Thus neither bird's final argument is well executed; their attacks flounder and their self-praise is undermined. The Nightingale's claim to teach 'Þat dusi luue ne last no3t longe' is as silly (considering the standard human reaction to her song) as the Owl's that her song is welcome to lonely wives. As the argument reaches its peak and focuses on those activities which cause men to kill the birds, it is thus made most ridiculous. Their preposterous failure to support their charges once more destroys any dignity or seriousness the conflict might have possessed. We are made aware yet again of the futility of argument and of its silliness.

The end comes suddenly in a squabble over the Owl's death, which, like the Nightingale's, has a 'once and future' quality. The Owl boasts that she helps men even after they have killed her, and the Nightingale insists that men's admittedly widespread desire to kill the Owl is to her discredit, and consequently she boasts of her own shame. 'Þu 3ulpest þat þu art manne loþ ... Þu 3ulpest of þire o3e schame' (1641, 1650). Of course the Owl does not really boast of men's hating her, only that she helps them despite their ill treatment. And since the Nightingale failed so signally to establish man's hatred as a discredit to the Owl, she cannot validly reintroduce the charge without backing it up with better arguments. Her 'victory' is self-declared and by no means logically established.

The poem's final movement (1653–1794), like the first, contains the threats of blows, but again the birds decide to prefer Nicholas's arbitration to combat, this time at the Wren's behest. And the final note struck is the praise of Nicholas and a plea for his preferment.

Viewing this poem simply as a debate, we have to agree that both birds turn in disgracefully incompetent performances. They argue in circles, their offensives are futile, the issues raised are left dangling aimlessly, while pressing charges are allowed to peter out. The birds are foolish and they make disputation look foolish. Such a result is not conducive to interpreting the poem as a reflection of a specific human debate on a serious topic. But then the contestants are only birds, a fact made especially clear by the sequential reading. Our initial impressions are built on details which seem purely avian. The first passage to hold much appeal for allegorists (the timing of the Owl's singing) does not come until line 323, and even that can legitimately be read in strictly avian terms. The first time the Nightingale is linked with lust (489–508), it is her own lust and that of animals around her, not human licentiousness. How can one keep allegorizing for any length of time a figure who, we are gleefully informed, sings behind privies and eats spiders, flies, and grubs (592–602)?

A massive proportion of the poem is cast in bird terms. Even the seemingly semi-human passages have a natural basis: owls did hunt mice in churches, and were stoned and hung on rods by farmers. Nightingales do return from migration in early spring, thus linking themselves by chance with rising sap and rutting, a link strengthened in men's minds by their singing at night. Even our final view of the birds – the little ones mobbing the Owl – is based on nature. A sequential reading shows us that such details are clustered especially thickly at the beginning, but they appear unflaggingly throughout. I suspect that the Owl's petty avian charges (575–602), which are lodged just as the arguments start getting serious, are a conscious contrivance for keeping the birds' avian nature clearly in our minds, lest we be led to take the troublesome issues too solemnly. To say that the author ever abandons these avian personalities for dogma is impossible; they never become mere mouthpieces.

A sequential reading also makes it plain that the poem is not haphazardly constructed. Many interpretations tacitly find the arguments chaotic and their course lacking discernible structure. Some scholars have done what they could to explain the fight by reference to various forms of debate: Atkins's legalistic scheme is one such attempt. To me though, the work does not appear to be structured according to a set of generic rules; its logic comes from within, not from without. The structure is what manipulates our view of the birds; in the course of the poem we are given three distinctly different perspectives on them. The perspective which demands the least personal involvement from the audience appears at the beginning (until roughly line 214) and end (from approximately line 1653 on). In these passages, especially the first, a narrator is present. He guides us into and out of the world of the birds, but also stands between the birds and us. Particularly in the first fifty or so lines, he enforces a distancing perspective by speaking in the past tense: 'was' (1, 5); 'sval' (7); 'seide' (9). This device lets him start the poem as if he intended to tell us of a curious adventure which had once befallen him – an effective method of introducing us into the fantasy world of the birds, but a concomitant result is to limit our emotional response.

Once the birds start to exchange acidulous comments, the narrator effaces himself. The birds are quoted directly, and we succumb to the illusion of hearing them ourselves. The sprinkling of 'she said's' and brief descriptions interfere with our rapport no more than do their equivalents in omniscient-narration novels; they are so conventional as to pass unnoticed. We respond freely to the birds, although since the issues they debate are relatively trivial, and they themselves are continually made ridiculous, our response is intellectual rather than emotional. The level of response demanded by this second perspective is that which characterizes most of the poem.

A third type of perspective is called for twice, in the passages centring on the birds' death (1045–1110; 1607–34). In these lines, the birds both speak in a queer 'once and future' manner of their own demises as if they had suffered such in the past, and might expect to do so again. The aim of this peculiar perspective may be to make us feel with particular urgency the plight of these victims of dispute. Quarrelling may result in death. This is a sobering point, and in some sense it lies at the heart of the whole poem. That the passages concerning their deaths are more important than has hitherto been recognized is suggested by the layout of the poem: about eight hundred lines, or *nearly half*, centre on adultery, prophecy, and related issues, the respective causes of each bird's death. This analysis of the varying narrative perspective should help make clear the development from a 'shallow' disengaged beginning, through a second stage in which we develop a lively *intellectual* interest in the birds, to two passages where an *emotional* response and sympathy are demanded. The poem is rounded off by a reverse progression away from the serious portions through the manoeuvrings of the technical victory and references to Nicholas of Guildford (which are of more intellectual than emotional interest) to a few final words by the narrator again, thus leading us out of the world of birds back again to our own world of men. The allusions to Nicholas and church politics aid the transition.

The inner movement of the poem is reflected in changing issues and a clearly calculated structure. From an elaborately inconsequential beginning which forcibly establishes the avian insignificance of the protagonists, the poem becomes gradually more serious in subjects, finally reaching the climaxes of the birds' deaths. Thereafter, the arguments change; our interest and concern ebb fast; and we gladly pass from the birds' tragedies to the everyday medieval world of job-hunting and church abuses.

Although the whole poem remains light and amusing, thanks to the birds' incompetence as debaters, special attention should be given to the heart and climax of the poem – the birds' deaths. Among the issues in this section are some which would be extremely serious in a *human* context, especially adultery and enticing to sin, witchcraft and senseless hatred. In the midst of the persiflage, these issues cause us only momentary concern and, because of the well-established avian context, even the murders of the birds (both caused by minor misunderstandings with men) bother us only temporarily. But we should take special note of what the author has done here. By presenting very serious issues in a markedly non-serious setting, he establishes a radical inconsistency between the subject and its vehicle. This incongruity is of no use to would-be allegorists – nor is the poem's sequence of arguments – but ridiculous disparity between subject and manner of presentation is a standard, indeed a defining feature of burlesque writing. Allegorically minded critics find a great deal in the poem that is serious, but are forced to ignore the low, amusing, avian setting. Far more plausibly, I think, one can see this setting as casting an ironic light on the serious issues. I pointed out earlier that the birds often seem to embody satiric commentary on mankind. Taking this point in conjunction with the disparity of subject and presentation, I propose next to offer a reading of the poem as a burlesque-satire on human contentiousness.

tbe potentialities of
Burlesque-satire
interpretation

Proving a work to be satiric is impossible on theoretical grounds if this
quality is not self-evident. Like allegory, sophisticated satire frequently
depends on an *unannounced* external referent, the butt or object of the
satire. When this is the case, a critic may deduce an eminently reasonable
satiric object, but he can never have the satisfaction of conclusive proof.
If Dryden had abandoned *Absalom and Achitophel* after writing his first
draft, and that manuscript, exact date and author unknown, were to turn
up in somebody's attic now, research might suggest that the events of the
early 1680s were the real concern of the poem, but we could never feel
positive, and inevitably some scholars would insist that the piece was
just a biblical poem written to capitalize on the success of *Paradise Lost.*
My assertion that *The Owl and the Nightingale* is a burlesque-satire may
seem initially unconvincing. Calling works satiric is just as modish (and
hence as suspect) as calling them ironic, and the likelihood of a sound
interpretation suddenly being discovered after all these years of study
may well seem small. Moreover, the label 'burlesque-satire' is modern –
the author would not have used it to describe his work. These drawbacks
are undeniable, but I hope that my awareness of such objections will in-
duce those critics who would raise them to give the burlesque-satire reading a fair hearing, for I believe that its advantages far outweigh its drawbacks. This approach can explain such nagging problems as the nature
and relevance of the birds' arguments, and the reason why this particular debate should seem a good recommendation of Nicholas of Guildford.

Definitions of satire are notoriously slippery and unsatisfactory. Authorities differ even on such basic issues as whether the mode should be called

destructive, static, or constructive in its vision.[1] Real trouble arises when one tries to fit all works called satire under a single umbrella definition. However, examining one example of the form and seeking to explain its effects by means of various definitions can be genuinely helpful. Hence I should like to introduce a number of comments on the theory of satire in the hope that their implications will make us more responsive to the features of *The Owl and the Nightingale*.

The simplest, least contestable definition of satire is that it *diminishes by means of ridicule*. 'The basic technique of the satirist is reduction: the degradation or devaluation of the victim by reducing his stature and dignity.'[2] Satire affects the relationship which would normally exist between reader or audience and the object being satirized. What the audience once viewed with admiration or at least took seriously, it is now encouraged to *look down upon*. This diminishing process can be applied to several kinds of object. (1) Characters in the work itself (only slightly distorted by caricature) can be ridiculed directly. An example is the women in Juvenal's sixth satire. (2) Characters in the work can serve as vehicles for satire really directed referentially at outside objects. Thus Dryden's Achitophel stands for Shaftesbury. (3) An idea or a behaviour pattern, instead of particular persons, may be the object of the attack. Huxley's *Brave New World* and Pope's *Rape of the Lock* are examples, respectively. In this more complex sort of satire, the characters may be foolish or contemptible, but the author's object in making them so has little to do with the individuals involved.

The Owl and the Nightingale best fits within this third category. I propose that the birds serve as vehicles for satire, that the referential equivalent is men quarrelling, and that the satiric object is human contentiousness. We laugh at the birds, but in themselves they do not constitute a meaningful butt since they are not diminished. They are already physically and morally negligible. Their role is to rouse amusement and contempt in the audience and direct those feelings towards the referential object.

In this respect the poem functions according to perfectly orthodox satiric theory. In satire, Hodgart tells us,

> criticism of the world is abstracted from its ordinary setting ...
> and transformed into a high form of 'play', which gives us both
> the recognition of our responsibilities and the irresponsible joy of

make-believe ... One recognizes true satire by this quality of 'abstraction'; wit and other technical devices ... are the means by which the painful issues of real life are transmuted. But even more important is the element of fantasy which seems to be present in all true satire. The satirist does not paint an objective picture of the evils he describes, since pure realism would be too oppressive. Instead he usually offers us a travesty of the situation, which at once directs our attention to actuality and permits an escape from it.[3]

As responsible members of a medieval community, we would not be amused by a nasty quarrel between a monk and a friar over practices of worship; we would take the men (and probably their fight) seriously. But shown an avian simulacrum of that fight, we can recognize its ludicrousness – and if the satire works, we may learn to transfer our newly won objectivity to the human equivalent.

Satire by itself does not, however, provide the critical vocabulary we need for *The Owl and the Nightingale*. It gives us *purpose*, but questions of *method* also arise. Here the definition of burlesque seems particularly apt – a process of *ridiculing by means of incongruous imitation*. Where animals concern themselves with human issues we have a situation ready made for incongruous imitation because of the disparity between subject and vehicle. In fact, it is exceedingly difficult for animals in quasi-human contexts to escape seeming to imitate man, thus commenting on him as well. Two colourless hawks might just manage to present a theological treatise without affecting our response, but let the identical words come from two geese, and no matter how serious and formal the treatise, we would always wonder if the goose's reputation for gabbling nonsense was meant as commentary on the subject matter being presented. A hint of character in an animal actor can utterly change our feelings about a work, and the Nightingale and Owl have exceedingly suggestive personalities. They are in fact ideal burlesque imitators of squabbling men: their avian nature keeps the quarrel from becoming too serious, and it provides many of the incongruities, delightful or disgusting, which diminish their human referents.

If satire is a diminishing through ridicule and burlesque a ridiculing through incongruous imitation, then I would call *The Owl and the Nightingale* a burlesque-satire which *diminishes its object through incongruous imitation*, the object being human contentiousness. The nature of the birds, their methods of arguing, their reactions to setbacks, and their attempts to gain advantages can all be seen as commentary on man's own proclivity for argument – in fact, as satiric commentary.

We can sharpen our understanding of *The Owl and the Nightingale* by considering some of the usual ramifications of satire. One is that the audience is made to feel superior. This is true of *The Owl and the Nightingale*: no listener feels that a bird is his equal. Birds are both smaller physically and lower in the scale of creation; thus we are not made uncomfortable by the indictment of man they act out. Our main reaction is amusement, although their quasi-human attributes may lead us eventually to more serious musings. Another quality of satire is humour; without humour, a supposed satire becomes mere railing, just as does a piece deficient in the fantasy element. The animal fantasy, however, is central to this poem, and the pervasive humour seems too obvious to need demonstration, but enough critics have tried to treat the debate as if it were genuinely serious to make insistence on the humour worthwhile.

Satiric works can generally be labelled 'punitive' or 'persuasive.'[4] Punitive satire deals harshly with its object, inviting contempt, scorn, disgust, and rejection. Though not totally negative – an ideal or at least an acceptable minimal positive standard is implicit – this type of satire is basically destructive in its aim. The persuasive mode tends to invite reform through laughter. The difference between audience and satiric butt is not as great; though the audience looks down on the satiric object, it will be able to see some likeness to itself. Characteristically, the persuasive type depicts men's faults as frailties or folly, not vicious depravity. *The Owl and the Nightingale*, in my opinion, is the latter kind of satire. 'Frailty' is extremely suggestive of the Middle English author's outlook and technique. He is not raging at man's depravity in the fashion popularized by Juvenal, Jerome, and Tertullian. This is not to say that his manner of poking fun is namby-pamby; he uses obscenity and scatology, traditional tools of the angry satirist, to attack some of men's cherished sexual vices. But overall, he seems to view man's weaknesses not as monstrous crimes or deliberate perversions, but as follies and stupidities. He is light-handedly whimsical or cheerfully sarcastic, not fanatically fervent.

David Worcester makes a comment which is revealing when applied to *The Owl and the Nightingale*: 'Burlesque-satire is historically the form developed for the informal observation of human nature and for the seemingly artless revelation of the writer's personality ... burlesque has long continued the natural vehicle for self-revelation in a whimsical way ...'[5] Despite the fact that the narrator is not a well-developed *persona* in *The Owl and the Nightingale*, scholars have responded warmly to what they divine as his personality and equitable temperament. His choice of subject and approach, his apparent leniency towards human frailties, and his sense of humour make a strongly favourable impression, even across the barriers of language and time. And if the author is Nicholas of Guildford, then the extravagant praise of himself which he puts in the birds' mouths is indeed likely to be somewhat whimsical, since self-commendation in these exaggerated terms seems incompatible with his obvious sense of the ridiculous. The use of satire to recommend its author is found elsewhere: Pope's 'Epistle to Dr Arbuthnot' exploits that combination non-whimsically, Swift's 'Verses on the Death of Dr Swift' whimsically. Indeed, any attempt to chide the sins of others implies that the author is above such weaknesses and therefore commendable. Juvenal's satires, by excoriating Roman society, extol himself and his high moral standards indirectly. I am not asserting that the author of *The Owl and the Nightingale* got the idea from Juvenal; Juvenal's satires are railing and bitter, and the medieval author would not have considered his own work a *satira*, but merely a humorous debate. Because he would not have used our critical term does not mean that he could not have discovered on his own the effectiveness of satiric perspective for commending the writer.

The nature of the satire rests on the relations between these birds and men. Clearly the poem is not wholly about birds as birds; there is too much talk about men, adultery, astrology, and the like for this to be a purely avian fable. But the fact that the birds never become just voices for human concerns is proof that this was not meant as a treatise whose narrators are peculiar but have no significance (e.g., hawks presenting theology). From the manner in which the birds are manipulated, there is strong evidence that we are meant to see a relationship between the birds and men in which men are ridiculed because they are sometimes silly enough to resemble these birds.

If the burlesque-satire interpretation can hope to win adherents, it must justify itself by accounting for the text better than other readings are able to do. I would like to consider therefore a number of problems which any interpretation has to handle. How does the author indicate his meaning? How and when might an audience deduce what the poem's concern is? How does the poem's structure fit a burlesque-satire interpretation? How are various issues relevant? Why should the birds' deaths be included? How does the birds' style of argumentation fit? How is the poem's ending meant to affect us? Plausible answers to these questions ought to make a burlesque-satire reading worth considering.

In trying to judge how and when the audience would realize the poem's purpose, one has to make the awkward admission that in this respect the author bungled. Had he made his point as clearly as we could wish, there would be no trouble telling what the poem was about and no significant divergence of critical opinion. However, any interpretation except Baugh's – that the poem is just two birds squabbling – has to allow that the author did not underline his point sufficiently, so this admission does not specifically damn a burlesque-satire reading; it damages all interpretations alike.

If we ask ourselves when contentiousness might suggest itself as the point of the poem, the answer is 'among our very earliest impressions and reactions': we wonder as we hear the first dozen lines whether legal disputation is under attack. The narrator tells us he heard a 'plait' (5), a 'plaiding supe stronge' (12). Sandwiched between these sober legal terms are the phrases 'aiþer aȝen oþer sval' and 'eiþer seide of oþeres custe / Þat alre worste þat hi wuste.' The incongruity in tone between the pithless formulas and the vivid descriptions is startling. The effect would be similar were an officially published résumé of a lawsuit to drop its dry diction and exclaim 'the lawyers screeched and jumped up and down, and the fat one's face turned purple before he burst forth with a stream of filthy accusations.' In both cases the juxtaposition of material with such different tonal quality results in the solemn pretensions of the official form being deflated. This combination seems to me to start the poem off in a manner suggesting sardonic disparagement of the 'plait.' We sense that the birds will be ridiculed, and may well anticipate even on rather slender evidence that the whole piece is meant to demonstrate that man's altercations deserve like sarcasm.

The notion that altercation itself is being disparaged is implicit in the layout of the first portion of the poem. Even if the listener has missed the suggestiveness of law term usage, he might respond to the types of arguments in the first three hundred or so lines, for it is here that the birds plunge into their most contemptible squabbles over manners, diet, looks, size, and habits. Even now, when formal belief in sin has fallen into desuetude, we acknowledge that boasting of one's looks is vain, taunting the natural appearance of others mean, and fighting over physical features the epitome of foolish vanity. Only the patent child-ishness of the birds keeps their words from being seriously distasteful. Because the issues are so nugatory, we hardly feel it worth our while to get worked up over them, but we do feel irritation, even disgust, that the birds should carry on in this fashion. I am arguing that the author's choice of topics directs our animus right from the outset towards quar-relling itself rather than specific issues. That focus is in keeping with a satire on human contentiousness.

Inability to pigeonhole the initial arguments in a one-to-one corre-spondence with human quarrels might also direct the listener to con-sider quarrelling itself the butt of the author's humorous derision. And that these arguments cannot be tied down is amply demonstrated by the efforts of the allegorists, who cannot agree on whether the 'real' concern is poetry, preaching, music, historical figures, or representatives of philo-sophies. Anyone can think up at least one such plausible referent as the poem proceeds, but the fair-minded will discard their hypotheses when the avian detail intrudes or the birds' stands contradict them. After a few false starts, such a listener might come to consider the possibility that the birds' squabbles are a reproach to *any* human quarrel so idiotic as to bear comparison with this one. Two women trying to upstage each other with finery are as silly as the poem's protagonists. So are members of two religious orders inveighing against each other's tonsure styles or habit colours. Disputes over poetry, preaching, and music would deserve our amused contempt to the precise degree in which they resemble the birds' quarrels. So would dispute over race or nationality or dietary re-strictions. Yet had the author tried to discredit any such 'serious' alter-cation directly, he might have failed to persuade us to view it dispas-sionately. Approaching human quarrelling through the birds teaches us to be more objective than we might otherwise have been.

Supposing that his hypothetical listener still has no inkling of the work's import, he is not likely to find a satisfactory answer to what the poem is about among the human issues alluded to directly: adultery, methods of preparing for life after death, the gift of prophecy, hatred, and jealousy. These add up to no easily discernible scheme, unless it is human quarrelling and its unpleasantly violent results, for that is the closest we can get to a common denominator for this group. The listener to whom contentiousness has not occurred by the time the poem is half over may just conclude, with Baugh, that these are two foolish birds involved in a silly quarrel. Such a poem would have little point. But just stating the nature of the poem in that bald manner might suggest to some that the birds stand for men, thus leading again to the notion that the poem is really about men's quarrelling. Thus even the most reductive description of the work should suggest the direction in which to turn for a more convincing explanation. As I admitted at the outset, the author did not make his point clearly enough, and that is a genuine flaw in the poem's construction. But burlesque-satire is implicit in a great many aspects of the work, including such basic ones as the poem's structure.

If the poem is a satire on human contentiousness, then its purpose presumably is to teach us to view the commonest types of human quarrelling objectively and see their inescapable foolishness.[6] This work's structure is perfectly designed to accomplish such a purpose. The change in perspective from disengaged amusement to emotional concern mirrors a development from the readily laughable issues at the beginning to those we are accustomed to take seriously like adultery and the unreasoning hatred felt towards one associated with unpleasantness. If the poem is at all successful in guiding our responses, we ought to learn to see through the birds' specious arguments, and recognize the fundamental foolishness of quarrelling as a solution to any problem, even when that quarrelling is invested with the trappings of solemnity. These lessons, of course, are as applicable to the affairs of men as they are to those of birds. For me, the poem succeeds in its endeavour to direct the reader's responses, but that is a personal valuation; anybody who disagrees must conclude either that my reading is mistaken or that the poem has failed in its objectives.

It would be an exaggeration to claim that the issues debated actively support the burlesque-satire reading, but they do not contradict or un-

dermine it. We do not automatically equate adultery or motives for singing or prophecy with contentiousness. It is the variety of the issues, the
refusal to focus on one sphere of activity, which makes them pertinent.
The avian activities mentioned include singing (to whom, where, why,
when), eating, habitat, nesting, family raising, deaths, relations to other
birds and to men. Human concerns mentioned directly or indirectly include traditional, learned, and religious wisdom; human habitats; causes
for celebration or mourning; adult and child toilet habits; and behaviour
between the sexes both in and out of marriage. The Owl's list of disasters
implies a whole range of human concerns – building ships, armies, material possessions, law and order, crafts, and agriculture. Miscellaneous
references to human activities include those to tools ('ovvel' 80), dyeing
('ipeint mid wode' 76), mill and cog wheel (86, 778), weaving and wool
(427 ff.), knightly dwellings ('Castel & burȝ' 766), knightly deeds (768),
knightly tools ('ȝerd & spure' 777), musical terms, legal terms, and politics and history ('king Henri'). These are catholic lists, and suggest that
the author did not intend to stress any one area of interest, either avian
or human. Had he meant the poem to be about any of the single subjects
proposed by allegorists, we would expect that subject to make its importance felt throughout, but no one topic enjoys that sort of pre-eminence,
a state of affairs consonant with satire on contentiousness in general, but
not with allegory.

Two issues, adultery and prophecy, do receive more attention than
we might anticipate, considering the unnegotiable nature of adultery
(granted Christian premises) and the rarity with which prophecy causes
mankind any trouble. The reason, of course, is that they are responsible
for the birds' deaths. The issues themselves do not matter, but rather
their harmful results. The birds are killed over minor misunderstandings:
the Owl does not cause the misfortunes she predicts, nor the Nightingale
adultery, as man in his fear, rage, or jealous resentment allows himself
to suppose. Their presence at such disasters is largely fortuitous. What is
significant is *man's* attitude – that a difference of opinion is enough to
justify killing the birds.

The author's use of the birds' deaths may be better understood when
recognized as a standard satiric technique with equivalents in many other
satires. Ronald Paulson has observed that there is what he calls a symbol
of violence 'at the center of almost every satire ... an image which, if
effective, the reader cannot easily forget.'[7] He cites the copulation of

woman and ass (Apuleius' *Metamorphoses*), half of Paris drowning in a flood of urine (Rabelais, *Gargantua*), the eating of children (Swift's *Modest Proposal*), and the threats of blinding and mastication in *Gulliver's Travels*. These events arise, he suggests, as a distillation of the corruption being attacked, or as a grotesque figuration of the logical consequences of the vice being objected to. The latter description seems relevant to these scenes in *The Owl and the Nightingale*. Their tone is less raucously ugly than those in *Metamorphoses* or *Gargantua*, and less disturbing to the imaginative reader than the Lilliputian threat of shooting arrows into Gulliver's eyes, because the actors are birds. But despite the slightly less violent impact achieved by our author, the Nightingale's dismemberment and the Owl's crucifixion are nonetheless 'symbolic actions that convey the central meaning of the satire,'[8] the evil results of quarrelling. The grim spirit of altercation often demands the death of one contestant. Man kills because that is part of quarrelling, even when he gains nothing from the birds' deaths. Disasters are not warded off by crucifying the Owl, or adultery by dismembering the Nightingale. I interpret the birds' slaughter simply as an object lesson on the results of quarrelling, proof of the evils inherent in contentiousness. As such, they are fittingly central to the poem, and our responses and emotional reactions are rightly focused upon them.

Not only do the birds' deaths make sense in a burlesque-satire context; their style of argumentation does too, and it is ill-explained by other approaches. The birds are blithering incompetents when it comes to debating, as I demonstrated in the last chapter. They are utterly incapable of following up telling points, of seeing through crooked arguments, even of thinking logically. They cannot in conscience be held up as serious apologists for any valued philosophy – they would put any serious stance to shame. Moreover, their self-contradictoriness is death to most allegorical readings: the Nightingale cannot be both layman and ecclesiast; the Owl cannot properly take the stand she does on wifely adultery. However, consistency and rhetorical skill are not requisite for a smooth reading if the poem is a satire on contentiousness. Indeed, inconsistency and incompetence are very suitable weapons for undermining the seriousness of the poem, and for conveying the impression that most disputation is foolish and pointless. When we stop to wonder how many human altercations are as ill-considered as this of the birds, we may well conclude that man would be better off could he curb his contentious spirit, or, if determined to dispute, should do so with as little fury as possible before a sympathetic arbiter prepared to do his best to compose the quarrel.

That we should learn to turn to arbitration rather than violence is, of course, exactly what the end of the poem points out. Death to contestants is no solution. Rather, they should ask Nicholas to decide. The conclusion of this piece thus directs us to the ostensible object of the poem – recommendation of Nicholas of Guildford. Relatively few interpretations are able to relate the text to the commending of Nicholas. How much of a recommendation for ecclesiastical preferment is a treatise on poetic style, with secular love poetry winning? Preaching styles and music are only a bit better. It is perfectly possible that Nicholas's stance or competence in any one such subject could be crucial to his getting preferment, but we are not told that he is involved in such activities at all. All we know about him is that he is skilled in judging, for the birds tell us as much:

> Þar he demeþ manie riȝte dom,
> An diht & writ mani wisdom,
> An þurh his muþe & þurh his honde
> Hit is þe betere into Scotlonde.
>
> (1755–8)

Clearly the author hopes Nicholas's pre-eminence in judging will win favour for him. A satire on foolish, ill-regulated contention is logical in a work whose aim is to recommend an arbitrator. Even the most successful satirist cannot realistically hope to shame everybody out of quarrelling. He may convince some high-minded individuals to review their own conduct and try to be less ready to clash when crossed. He may also make some see that particular causes they espouse do not deserve such fierce feeling. Were the satire to do even that much, it would be more successful than most. A satirist might reasonably hope to persuade some listeners to prefer arbitration to fisticuffs (whether free-for-all or formalized into trial by combat); and that, it seems to me, is one of the aims of the poem, an aim laudatory in its own right, as well as suitable for recommending a man whose talent is composing squabbles.

Taken all in all, the burlesque-satire approach to the poem has much to recommend it. This interpretation lacks the certainty which explicit comment by the poet might have supplied, but then so do all readings. In other respects, the approach seems to excel rival interpretations in its ability to account for the text. None of the peculiarities, like the debate's lack of resolution, throw the reading into question. The birds' incompetence, inconsistency, and stands on specific issues are all appropriate. So are the development of the arguments, the structure, the climactic deaths, and the conclusion. The ability to handle so many problematical features makes the interpretation deserving of consideration at least, even if its terminology seems unhistorical.

The burlesque-satire reading first recommended itself to me when I was trying to understand to what extent the birds' arguments were meant to be taken seriously, and how the humour was supposed to affect audience response. When reading patristic or other serious-minded interpretations, one keeps wanting uncomfortably to ask 'Why are birds the spokesmen?' and more particularly, 'Why such *silly* birds?' Two other recent critics have been moved by this same uneasiness.[9] John Gardner and Constance Hieatt were the first to employ satire and burlesque terminology on this poem, and both far surpass previous scholars in sensitivity to the poem's unserious surface.[10] Hieatt's discussion of the birds' illogic and Gardner's of their humour are illuminating, and should be taken into account by all future critics. But even as Peterson and Donovan started with the same patristic material yet arrived at different conclusions, so too Gardner, Hieatt, and I diverge, the parting of ways coming at a key stumbling-block – the identification of the object of the satire. To those not accustomed to thinking of *The Owl and the Nightingale* as primarily funny, my attempts to draw distinctions between three interpretations with similar viewpoints may seem like hairsplitting. The differences are real, however, and affect the readings' ability to encompass all the problematical features of this work.

Gardner reads the poem as a burlesque on the literary debate tradition rather than on the general sin of quarrelling. Why should that be any the less satisfactory an object of satire? Gardner spends much of his article showing that the birds are meant to be funny, and in this he succeeds brilliantly. He provides excellent proof of the point, and his discussion should carry conviction even to those accustomed to a conven-

tional approach. However, he never shows how this comic humour sur-
rounding the birds makes the *genre* the object of the satire, rather than
the birds themselves or the causes they espouse. In fact, he never explores the mechanics of satire or burlesque at all, and this omission
leads to some weaknesses in his argument. He calls the poem a 'joke on
the debate genre' because some characteristics of debate – conflict, types
of subject, resolution – are handled comically. But comic handling of
these elements as he describes it need only make this an amusing debate,
not one whose *form* is being made fun of.

Literary forms are defined by varying criteria. Some are labelled primarily according to content, as are the heroic plays of the Restoration
or the picaresque or gothic novel. Others are recognized by their format:
the epistolary novel, the sestina, and the debate. Burlesques of the for-
mat-defined genres are rare, but when attempted, they are usually executed by means of a perfectly normal layout whose absurdities and
shortcomings are pointed out by means of incongruous subject matter.
To burlesque a sestina, one would *have* to preserve the form if the satire
were to be meaningful. One would use hopelessly awkward and unnatural word order and strained sense to demonstrate the shortcomings of
so rigid a word scheme. In *Shamela*, the form of the epistolary novel is
ridiculed when Shamela gives a blow by blow account of attempted rape
in the present tense. Logically it would be unsound for a satirist to de-
form a generic format for purposes of mockery. How can he prove the
original to be at fault if he introduces formal faults himself? For this
poem to be a burlesque of the debate form, we would expect the author
to build a normally structured debate about a preposterous subject. De-
pending on how you read *The Owl and the Nightingale*, it has no subject
or many subjects, but neither is an effective means of discrediting debate,
compared, for example, to debating whether or not fleas have the right
to bite men. Nor does *The Owl and the Nightingale* reach a preposterous
conclusion, the other appropriate characteristic of a burlesque on the debate as a form. When a king and somebody representing a river seriously
debate the river's right to flood each spring, and the king wins, and all
the town triumphantly celebrates the fact that there will be no more
floods, then the right of debate to be taken seriously is called into
question. *The Owl and the Nightingale* does not work in this fashion.
Its lack of conclusion is no genuine indictment of the debate form, for
debates exist for their conclusions, and most debates reach resolutions

of some sort. But lack of resolution does discredit quarrelling, by suggesting that either it cannot reach a conclusion, or that it can do so only with violence or arbitration.

Gardner's explanation is thus somewhat at odds with the poem. He regards the birds as humorous embodiments of Nicholas's wild youth and his current self, notable for sobriety and trustworthiness. To some extent, this is certainly likely, but it cannot be taken far. If the birds are considered extensions of Nicholas in any serious fashion (as Gardner seems inclined to do, p. 8), their illogic and style of quarrelling is not much of a recommendation. Nor is it easy to see how debunking the debate form would help Nicholas in his job-seeking, whereas a debunking of quarrelling, especially quarrelling without an arbiter, can have direct bearing on Nicholas's situation, since his qualifications for preferment seem to be judicial.

Constance Hieatt looks to a different object of satire: 'it is not just a parody of the form but a satire on human nature' (p. 159). Obviously this reading comes close to my own, but 'human nature' seems excessively general to serve as a satiric butt. If all human nature (or even just all that is bad) is the object, how can the poem work as a satire? What kind of reform can be expected in response? Does the poem even turn an analytic eye on a representative spread of human nature? The range of personality types and attitudes which are paraded during the poem is not overly wide. Though we would not expect virtuous or saintly outlooks to be present, we might expect their hypocritical counterfeits to be present, but they are absent except for the Owl's holier-than-thou stance. So are indolence, avarice, and gluttony. Relatively little real wickedness appears. The birds display their own rather trivial characters and they quarrel. All human stances which cannot be represented by that conjunction fall outside the scope of the poem. True, variations in character – gloomy and cheerful, learned (after a fashion) and unlearned – give us some sense of the variety of human responses possible in a conflict, but when we remember this limiting factor, *conflict*, we can see to how great an extent the poem is really about quarrelling. The admirable qualities in human nature cannot appear because they are incompatible with such squabbling. Only those characteristics contributing to bickering, boasting, and malicious accusations enter – such as vanity, unfairness, aggressiveness, and petulance. These are nasty faults, but seem relatively shallow and ordinary compared to the many evils which man can perform. This relatively narrow range of human characteristics seems to me to support the idea that the burlesque relationship between birds and men is limited to man's contentiousness rather than to human nature in general.

Hieatt's reading is able to meet most of the objections levelled at other readings. The number of subjects raised is no problem, nor is the inconclusive ending. The debate form is not directly relevant, but it does not contradict her thesis. The relevance of this poem to Nicholas of Guildford's plea for preferment is again less direct than that which I propose. But there are two basic objections to the theory of general satire on human nature, and I think they prove decisive. First, only a relatively narrow spread of human nature appears in the poem. Second, what would be the point? To satirize the unalterable is silly. Are we to take *The Owl and the Nightingale* as the *jeu d'esprit* of a witty nihilist?

There remains the problem of how likely the burlesque-satire reading is historically. Burlesque-satire after all is a modern term, and *satira* to the author probably meant Juvenal, or what Peter calls 'complaint.' This is an awkward question, and my answer can be no more than tentative. To begin with, I know of no work of similar scope and aim until the *Nun's Priest's Tale* (written between one and a quarter to two centuries later) where animal antics satirically burlesque a human weakness, vanity. In all probability we must credit the author of *The Owl and the Nightingale* with a virtuosity unique for his time, and that makes us uncomfortable, for *lusus naturae* are hard to fit into literary theories. On the other hand, almost every other interpretation of *The Owl and the Nightingale* assumes its uniqueness without ever acknowledging the problems of that assumption: Anne Baldwin, for instance, adduces no contemporary examples of similarly elaborate, sophisticated political allegory. And since some critics are aware of the unusual amount of humour in the poem, I hope they will at least grant the possibility of further unusualness. This is not to claim that the author has created absolutely *ex nihilo*: fables offer innumerable examples of animals used to mock single human vices by means of incongruous imitation. Although the fables are short, as a rule, they may well have provided the author of *The Owl and the Nightingale* with some of his ideas. Indeed, though I suspect he viewed his own production merely as a humorous debate (*altercatio*), he may have found inspiration in the fables for that feature which distinguishes *The Owl and the Nightingale* from other debates –

the ebullient gusto of the protagonists and their informal, free-wheeling interaction.

If the burlesque-satire approach can be expected to supersede others, it must prove more successful than they at explaining some of the problems inherent in the poem. I believe it is capable of doing just that. The use of debate genre for commendatory purpose, for instance, is no longer an inexplicable authorial vagary. We can easily understand why Nicholas should be carefully considered for any kind of job which would bring him into contact with informal or formal quarrels, if he is as expert at resolving contentions as these exemplars of strife firmly believe him to be. If the object of the satire is human contentiousness and the silliness and tragedy resulting from that trait, then Nicholas's value should indeed seem great, for we are allowed to see what he is expert at settling. We, of course, are viewing a comic distortion of the broils he can quiet, but we are reminded often enough during the poem of the realities of man's world to keep in mind Nicholas's real value. If the concern of the poem were really the specific issues, then we might conclude that Nicholas felt himself competent in the peculiar range of subjects mentioned, but not much else. If, however, our interest is directed not to the particulars but to quarrelling in the abstract, then Nicholas's powers are markedly enhanced.

The author's decision to cast the poem with birds as protagonists is explicable when we consider the demands of burlesque-satire. It is through the use of birds that he achieves his burlesque effects. Because of their smallness and lowness in the scale of creation, they diminish any human stance equivalent to their own. The mechanics of satiric diminution are similarly accomplished in Book One of *Gulliver's Travels.* That the Lilliputian prince should pride himself on his height is ridiculous to us because his advantage over his courtiers is so insignificant by our standards that it could scarcely be measured. Likewise the birds' fierce antagonism based on diet seems to us to be over a distinction without difference. In *Gulliver*, we also see satiric diminution accomplished through transfer from one cultural context to another. Big and Little Endians are the Lilliputian equivalent to Catholics and Protestants; trilling and hooting the equivalents to two styles of outlook whether expressed as preaching, singing, poetry writing, or approach to religion. The result of such 'cultural' transformation is ridicule in each case. Swift's satiric techniques and their effects have long been recognized.

Oddly, the same techniques have long passed unnoticed in *The Owl and the Nightingale.*

Many pieces of the puzzle seem to fall into place of their own accord if we read the poem as a burlesque-satire whose satiric object is human contentiousness. The use of birds rather than men as debaters satisfies that form's need for 'low' characters at whom we can laugh. Once we have laughed at them and their concerns, then we are obliged to admit that our automatically serious response to the human equivalents may be mistaken. The spectrum of arguments, as well as their essential inconclusiveness, can also be explained by this approach. The range of types of issues lets us find rough equivalents to numerous human arguments. Their triviality, of course, discredits argumentation by showing its pointlessness, as does the lack of resolution to the whole debate. Furthermore, this ending directs our attention to the man who is supposed to be able to end the quarrel, Nicholas of Guildford. Other interpreters have generally had trouble finding unity in the apparent disparity of bird debate and plea for promotion. Why should such a debate, which does not even tell us Nicholas's opinions, be a good means of recommendation? The best explanation is not, as some have argued, that the debate displays his interests, but rather that it shows up the pointlessness and ugly results of quarrelling, and it forms a tribute to a man who can help eliminate such altercations.

NOTES

1 Representative formulations of these views are found respectively in Samuel Marion Tucker, *Verse-Satire in England before the Renaissance* (New York: Columbia University Press 1908) 5; John Peter, *Complaint and Satire in Early English Literature* (Oxford: Clarendon Press 1956) 56; and Thrall, Hibbard, and Holman, *A Handbook to Literature* (1936; rev. ed. New York: Odyssey Press 1960) 436.

2 Matthew Hodgart, *Satire*, World University Library (New York: McGraw Hill 1969) 115

3 Hodgart, pp. 11–12

4 The terms are Edward W. Rosenheim, Jr's, in *Swift and the Satirist's Art* (Chicago: University of Chicago Press 1963) 14 ff.

5 David Worcester, *The Art of Satire* (Cambridge, Mass.: Harvard University Press 1940) 54

6 I am not arguing that the author is condemning all contention. Christianity recognizes as righteous wrath directed against evil. The sharp snubs of the

Pearl Maiden or of Chaucer's parson, even followed by action, would have seemed justifiable, and the author would presumably have supported good against evil were the two sides clearly divisible. But few ordinary human quarrels can claim such moral absolutism.

7 Ronald Paulson, *The Fictions of Satire* (Baltimore: The Johns Hopkins Press 1967) 9

8 Paulson, p. 10

9 John Gardner, '*The Owl and the Nightingale*: A Burlesque' *PLL* 2 (1966) 3–12, and Constance Hieatt, 'The Subject of the Mock-Debate Between the Owl and the Nightingale' *SN* 40 (1968) 155–60

10 Following the lead of Gardner and Hieatt, Jay Schleusener (*MP* 70 [1973]) also analyses humour in the poem, especially as it relates to the birds' irreconcilability.

8

conclusions

Two general questions remain to be answered: why was a plea for pre-ferment cast in the form of a burlesque-satire debate, and how well does the burlesque-satire reading stand up to the objections I levelled earlier at other interpretations? The former involves us in questions about self-recommendation, patronage, job-seeking, and audience response to the poem. The latter demands some recapitulation of points already made, but is necessary because of my harsh critiques of the efforts of others. In fairness to those critics, I must submit my own construct to the same scrutiny.

That this poem is to some degree a plea for preferment is generally accepted. Critics differ and probably always will on whether that aim was incidental or central, on whether entertainment or commendation was the author's primary concern, because such qualitative judgments are not susceptible of proof. My belief that commendation was central is therefore a personal assessment, and not everyone will agree. I should like to discuss the critical potential of this view, along with that of a corollary assumption that Nicholas was the author, because together they seem to provide the best answers to questions still besetting the poem. If the author was someone other than Nicholas, the indirect, whimsical, and sketchy nature of the commendation would be difficult to account for. If Nicholas is the author, this feature makes sense, for serious self-praise, without distancing or disguise, would have been vir-tually impossible in a culture whose writing conventions demanded that a writer assume a very modest pose if he mentioned himself at all.[1]

If one feels the poem's aim to have been simple entertainment, then one need not question its form, for entertaining it certainly is. If the poem is a plea, however, there remains a question of why *this* poem was produced for *that* purpose. What is the relationship between the entertainment which the poem offers and Nicholas's deserts? David Worcester's comment that burlesque-satire is whimsically self-revealing of the author seems to me to provide the key. That which pleases and entertains us in this particular poem happens to be evidence of the qualities and qualifications which would recommend Nicholas for preferment.

For instance, the author shows an uncanny ear for the cadence of a quarrel. His poem is amazing in its virtuosity in handling different quarrel idioms. When the two birds commence hostilities, they sound like children: the sing-song tone, the 'you-make-me-sick' attitude (39), the stress on physical ugliness and dirtiness (91-6) can be heard if Catholic and Protestant children fight, or Christian and Jewish. Ignorance, vague fears, misunderstandings, and misinterpretations of habits abound in the opening lines, and again when the Nightingale talks about men in the North (1004-14), who eat raw meat and drink milk and look as if they came from Hell! Children in such fights are often cruel, and the Nightingale excels herself in nastiness when she describes the owlet's befouling the falcon's nest (the misdemeanour is even a childhood one), the tattletale report of the falcon fledglings, and the terrifying anger of the adult bird. Anyone familiar with quarrels that occur on this level and concern such subjects will feel an amused recognition that Nicholas 'knows what he is talking about' when he sets the altercation in motion.

His ability to catch the tonal characteristics of another type of quarrel is demonstrated by the birds' repeated use of 'King Alfred says.' That worthy is invoked no less than twelve times.[2] The first time he appears, we may be tempted to admire the Nightingale's learning, but as the occurrences mount, the invocation gets funnier each time. The birds remind one of all the arguers one has heard who cannot think out a position and who substitute an authority for thought. Whether they cite King Alfred, Confucius, Chairman Mao, their bishop, their husband, or an idolized friend who knows *everything*, the result is the same: the mental stature of the debater is reduced, especially when, as here, only one authority is cited. (Backing a complex argument with references to evidence and appropriate authorities is another matter.) The birds are by and large desperately unoriginal arguers, and we are made to feel this and see their similarities to their less excusable human counterparts in this use of authority. The citations, after all, are the most banal of platitudes.

The histrionic properties of the poem have never received much attention. They are considerable, however, and I suspect that if the poem were imaginatively narrated, audience laughter would be encouraged in a manner that would dispose the audience in Nicholas's favour, were he indeed known to be the author. The exaggerated tonal contrasts and flights of rhetoric are cases at point. The anaphoric passages (1005 ff., 1154 ff., and 1191 ff.) would give any vivid reader great scope. The Owl's torrent of self-congratulation in lines 1191-1206, all but three of which begin with 'Ich wot,' would be perfect for comic 'business.' The Owl is *so* pleased with the number and range of the disasters she can predict. She could be portrayed as starting pompously, then (after line 1201) as speeding up in an effort to deliver the rest of this resounding masterlist in one breath that its majestic cadence not be broken. Her collapse at the list's end, and her exhausted 'An ʒet ich con muchel more' would deflate her pretensions both to knowledge and her egotistical rhetoric. If citations to Alfred were delivered with pompous complaisance, they too would invite laughter, laughter which is not scornful and harsh, but warm and shared between audience and author. This sense of shared amusement would encourage good will towards Nicholas.

The shared amusement would also be encouraged in some of the poem's contrasts, the most striking of which is the Nightingale's exalted portrayal of herself as kingpin in the world's enjoyment of spring, followed by the Owl's gloss on this text. The Owl presents the Nightingale's eagerness in song as equivalent to that of a churl in his hasty and impulsive rutting (507-22). We can laugh at this mockery of the Nightingale's pretensions, and at the Owl for her prurient imagination. Often we laugh with the birds at such subjects as the folly of adulterers, as well as at the birds for their illogic and ineptitude in their discussion of the matter. For all that we look down on the birds, we enjoy them too much to reject them for their faults. This dual perspective of amused liking and contempt would be the natural response to most narrative interpretations of the poem, but would be especially encouraged by a dramatic reading which stressed the poem's humorous possibilities. Different readers would wring different effects from the same passage: the

Nightingale's lines on human adultery (1473 ff.) could be spoken in tones of outrage, or genuine puzzlement; but perhaps funniest would be her repeating the arguments earnestly and solemnly by rote, as a child repeats half-comprehended warnings from its mother, or a student the teachings of a professor. The narrator could augment the Nightingale's lack of genuine comprehension around line 1496 by having her grope for the next line, possibly thrown off stride by audience laughter, and then have her 'remember' and go on in a hasty, self-conscious rush, the words tumbling out over each other so as to bring out the garbled senselessness of her argument.

All of these features of the poem's surface and presentation invite audience laughter. We are encouraged to laugh at the birds, the human issues, and at the quarrelling itself. We are given the sense that Nicholas can hate the sin while loving the sinner, because he can see and present the humorous as well as the serious side of their quarrel. We can believe the birds when they say Nicholas is a good judge, as they do in lines 1755–8:

Þar he demeþ manie riȝte dom,
An diht & writ mani wisdom,
An þurh his muþe & þurh his honde
Hit is þe betere into Scotlonde.

One who can keep a humorous, warm, but morally proper view of quarrelling would deserve consideration for preferment. Since his judicial qualifications are what he apparently wishes to be counted in his favour, the choice of the debate-form – a quarrel – is a logical means for Nicholas to proclaim his virtues indirectly. He can show how the fight heats up dangerously towards violence, and how it gets nowhere because no arbiter is present to untangle the arguments and find a solution.

If we view the work in this fashion – primarily as recommendation for a practiced arbitrator, secondarily as a satire on quarrelling set up in order to praise that arbitrator indirectly – all sorts of pieces fall into place. The various folk, literary, and religious traditions concerning the birds are not used to project philosophical messages, but are merely natural sources for the birds' boasts and taunts. Where else could the author have turned for avian information? There would be no point to inventing charges not usually associated with the birds – that the Owl drank too much for example or that the Nightingale pilfered from the church alms box – because an audience would have trouble assessing the validity of such charges and boasts. As it is, the listeners can gain a great deal of amusement from seeing through the birds' subterfuges and watching them twist their material to make a charge more damaging or a personal trait more exalted.

The unusual choice of the debate form for a recommendation is explained by the author's necessarily indirect approach to his primary concern – commendation of himself. His decision to use animal protagonists is explained by his satiric attitude towards quarrelling. They are a natural means for creating the proper audience response – amused contempt – because they are 'low.' Why these particular species of birds were chosen remains completely conjectural. As Gardner and others have pointed out, these birds may have held private meanings for Nicholas. When the Nightingale proposes Nicholas as judge, the Owl answers:

Ich granti wel þat he us deme,
Vor þeʒ he were wile breme,
& lof him were niʒtingale
& oþer wiʒte gente & smale,
Ich wot he is nu suþe acoled;
Nis he vor þe noʒt afoled,
Þat he for þine olde luue
Me adun legge, & þe buue.
Ne schaltu neure so him queme
Þat he for þe fals dom deme.
He is him ripe & fastrede,
Ne lust him nu to none unrede:
Nu him ne lust na more pleie,
He wile gon a riʒte weie.

(201–14)

The Owl seems to be saying that though Nicholas may once have been somewhat libertine, she believes him to be a reformed character, capable of filling a responsible post without bringing any discredit or scandal upon it. Identification of the birds as spokesmen for an old and new Nicholas throughout the poem, like any other allegorical reading, runs afoul of the avian detail. But in this one passage the two certainly seem to have personal significance which may have contributed to their being chosen. Other possible reasons include their natural opposition as figures of gloom and cheer, and their similarly mixed and contradictory traditions.

We might wonder why there are no extended allusions, whether direct or allegorical, to contemporary events or current intellectual contexts, why indeed such references are so lacking that none can be found to date the poem. Why does the author not inform his prospective patron about his views on important issues? One possibility is that Nicholas feared that his opinions were not those considered desirable. Since, we gather, he has been thwarted in his rise, he might want to be careful not to take any chance of offending a patron. However, the refusal to display Nicholas's opinions may be even more central to the design of the poem than fear of giving offence. If Nicholas is being touted as a judge, his reputation is enhanced if he does not display biases and appears impartial. In this case the absence of personal detail and opinion would be explicable in terms of both the poem's purpose and the awkwardness of self-praise.

We may wonder also why the poem was written in English. Possibly it was intended for reading aloud to a general audience. Gottschalk envisions it as read to English commoners, and Russell as presented to the patron by means of a public reading. If the poem is twelfth century, then it might be that Nicholas was intent upon proving his own fluency in English to show that he could deal with English litigants. As a cleric (he is called 'Maister' 191), he was barred by papal decree from serving as a justice in a secular court system after 1179. Nonetheless, English would have been useful to an officer of either an ecclesiastical court or an episcopal *ménage*. And, of course, English may have been the language favoured by the hoped-for patron.

About this patron we can guess very little. An ecclesiastical superior is the most likely a priori, but the author is rather too outspoken about church abuses for that deduction to seem certain. A bishop would have needed a good sense of humour to respond favourably to an aspirant who asserts:

'He naueþ bute one woning.
Þat his bischopen muchel schame,
An alle þan þat of his nome
Habbeþ ihert, & of his dede.
Hwi nulleþ hi nimen heom to rede
Þat he were mid heom ilome,
For teche heom of his wisdome,
An ӡiue him rente a uale stude
Þat he miӡte heom ilome be mide?'
  'Certes,' cwaþ þe Hule, 'þat is soð,
Þeos riche men wel muche misdoð
Þat leteþ þane gode mon,
Þat of so feole þinge con,
An ӡiueþ rente wel misliche,
An of him leteþ wel lihtliche;
Wið heore cunne heo beoþ mildre
An ӡeueþ rente litle childre:
Swo heore wit hi demþ a dwole,
Þat euer abid Maistre Nichole.'

(1760-78)

Nicholas is sufficiently cautious in expressing his opinions on controversial issues that we might expect him to avoid such a blast at bishops were the poem intended for one. But the recipient may have been a noble, or even the king. Though no longer able to hand out livings directly, such magnates were still powerful enough to influence elections and manipulate the official channels of appointment.

The patron and the reasons for writing in English remain conjectural. I believe, however, that Nicholas of Guildford's authorship can be spoken of as probable. Though not susceptible to proof, this hypothesis is supported by strong circumstantial evidence. The indirect nature of the praise, its whimsical exaggerations ('þurh his honde / Hit is þe betere into Scotlonde,' 1757-8), as well as the care and skill clearly devoted to the making of the poem all fit Nicholas's authorship, and all equally militate against the idea of the author's being merely a friendly advocate. Even the dialect – probably the Guildford region – supports this hypothesis. The selection of the birds may reflect Nicholas's claim to be a reformed character; their quarrelling as well as their agreement on his virtues form a tribute to him and his professed qualifications – a more effective case than boasting, but less direct than one would expect from an enthusiastic friend. And, of course, if Nicholas is the author, the poem's humane outlook, warm humour, and sane rejection of dispute make a very fine recommendation indeed.

If the reader were to compile a list of the observations, objections, and warnings of a theoretical nature which I have directed at other critical approaches, that reader would possess a handy aid to further study of the poem. The separate points, though minor, test the adequacy of various facets of a reading, and added up, they constitute a kind of Siege Perilous for judging the worth of the whole. But that list would be scrappy and exceedingly cumbersome to use: many of the remarks, after all, were aimed at specific transgressions against theory or logic. For their full potentiality to be available to others, specific applicability will have to be translated into general terms. And indeed I believe that their essential value can be condensed into three touchstones, corresponding to the three avenues of approaching the poem dealt with in Chapters 2 through 5 – one relating to the protagonists' avian nature, one to the literary form, and the third to the type of reading the poem demands. After describing these three tests and making their implications as clear as I can, I will measure the burlesque-satire reading against them.

That the poem alludes to many traditions regarding owls and nightingales, and that those traditions contradict each other, is fact. *Both birds are the inheritors of favourable and unfavourable lore.* How the critic uses this motley material to estimate the birds' characters is the first critical test. Common practice has been to regard the Owl as a Christian ascetic and therefore good, while the Nightingale has been variously interpreted as natural man (Hässler), siren singer of sensuality (Robertson and Peterson), and chorister of divine love (Donovan). None of these critics justifies his choosing among diverse traditions, yet any interpretation dependent on selection *must* justify its choice. In so far as I can judge, there is no way whatever to prove the correctness of a selection; the author does not favour either bird with a more logical stance or give a genuine triumph to either. As I have demonstrated in Chapter 6, both are ridiculed and both remain mixed in character. Readings which try to exalt either bird, unless they can marshal supporting evidence never before found, are invalid.

The second incontrovertible fact is the poem's generic form. *The Owl and the Nightingale* is a debate, and that information automatically raises two questions: (a) *What is the issue debated?* and (b) *Who wins?* Since the formal purpose of a debate is to reach resolution on an issue, these responses are absolutely natural and logical, and the wrong answers to them expose flaws in an interpretation. The issue at stake has been variously identified as styles of poetry writing, preaching, or music; astrology; and specific human political antagonisms. None of these can encompass the wealth of low avian detail however. 'Service to mankind,' which does become the birds' concern as the poem progresses, is of no genuine interest to man (and hence no justification for the poem), and as a subject it is too illogically argued to make it appear the sort of school-exercise topic which dominates Ermoldus Nigellus' *Carmen* or Sedulius Scotus' *Certamen*. General outlook readings, which identify the birds as 'gaiety and gravity,' or 'art and philosophy,' make 'way of life' a kind of subject, but that too is unable to account for vast stretches of avian detail and the illogical argumentation. No one, in fact, has been able to extract from the birds' squabbles a single issue which would give the poem a plausible *raison d'être*. This state of affairs exists because *there is no meaningful subject*; the birds' debate is pointless. That does not mean that the poem is pointless. *The birds' concerns must not be confused with the author's.*

The question of who wins has been answered in every conceivable way: Atkins awards the prize to the Nightingale, Peterson and Robertson to the Owl, Kincaid and Donovan grant both equal goodness, Kinneavy prefers equal faultiness. As I have shown in Chapter 3, victory has not yet been awarded validly, and indeed to do so is impossible. The same absence of positive evidence which makes selecting among traditions impossible destroys our chance of proving one triumphant. Hence any reading which favours one bird cannot be accepted. This test point, along with that concerning the subject, eliminates quite a number of interpretations.

The third test concerns the method of reading demanded by the poem. Those critics unable to find a subject for debate in the birds' actual words turn to allegory, thereby importing a subject from outside the poem. This technique may be labelled unsound on both practical and theoretical grounds: practical, because few of the attempts have been plausible enough to win more adherents than the original proposer; theoretical because the texture of the poem is so avian that huge amounts of it will not allegorize well, and those portions would function as a constant distraction from the allegory. Moreover, the poem lacks the clear moral or message usual in an allegorical fable. Though allegory cannot be utterly ruled out on theoretical grounds, the evidence against it is strong.

The reading which calls the poem a burlesque-satire on human contentiousness seems to me to stand up well to these three touchstone questions. It makes no selection among the avian traditions. Though they contribute some of the poem's humour, no single one need be taken into account for the interpretation to be valid. Indeed, the audience could enjoy the poem without prior knowledge of even so elementary a fact as the Nightingale's association with love because the birds themselves tell us all we need to know. The interplay of personalities, which is what galvanizes the debate to the pitch we find so entertaining, is based on traditions, essentially because that is what the birds turn to for their material. A person knowledgeable in the lore will recognize the appropriateness of the charges and accusations, but most of the pleasure of seeing through the birds' manoeuvres is available to anyone with a sense of logic. Moreover, the dual strand of good and bad traditions contributes directly to a burlesque-satire reading since the bad always serve to undermine the good, and thus provide the ammunition to deflate comically many of the birds' grand claims to merit. Mixed characters in a poem present no problem for a burlesque reading.

The burlesque-satire approach likewise survives the touchstone of generic problems well. That the birds' argument should be pointless is perfect for a satire on quarrelling; what better way to show up the uselessness of biased and spiteful contention than portray it going nowhere and achieving nothing? This approach does not confuse the author's concerns with that of the birds: hence it can accommodate with ease a debate without a central, unifying issue. The author's concern is to debunk quarrelling, the birds' is to quarrel. The nature of the issues is irrelevant in a burlesque-satire reading, so low avian detail and astrology or adultery can jostle each other without destroying the interpretation. Nor does this approach demand that one be acclaimed winner. If quarrelling is to be debunked, it is imperative that there be no victor; otherwise a listener might conclude that something – victory and concomitant supremacy – could be gained by quarrelling. The author's leaving affairs so ambiguous and unsettled is but a technique to reveal the frustration pursuant upon this kind of argument.

The burlesque-satire approach to the poem demands no importation of meaning, just identification of the satiric object. Imposition of a pattern from outside the poem is a method engendered by despair at making sense of the birds' quarrel. But if we do not look to their issues for the purpose of the poem, we need not seek an external context to explain it. The explanation is contained within the poem if we realize that the birds are meant to quarrel pointlessly. The author's purpose is to expose the futility of arguing without an arbiter, because he wishes to pay compliment to the value of a skilled judge who happens to need a job. This pattern is self-contained, and it accounts for all parts of the poem.

What kind of poem confronts us in *The Owl and the Nightingale*? In the most fundamental terms, it is a debate, albeit one lacking clear resolution; also an animal poem with ebulliently avian protagonists. Even though many of the avian activities mentioned seem sufficiently parallel to human concerns to suggest comparison, they all are firmly grounded in nature or bird lore – none is a purely human concern inserted lamely as a pseudo-avian interest. When human issues are mentioned, they are handled directly – men's getting to heaven, wifely adultery, and the human rage that causes the birds' deaths are all clearly treated as human issues, not disguised as avian problems. And one human concern, which receives prominent treatment, is, of course, the poverty and neglected merit of Nicholas of Guildford.

There is considerable diversity here, a diversity which defies many of the techniques normally applied to the poem. Critics have tried to read it by seizing on a single minor point, one issue mentioned in passing like astrology, or one allegorically relevant debate like that over types of poetry. The critic who settles on one such topic ought to ask himself how much of the poem is directly concerned with the one point. Whatever the issue may be, even singing, I think he will have to admit that it occupies relatively few lines. And if the chosen issue is essentially human, he has to wonder to what extent the low avian detail interferes with serious purpose. To put such a reading forth, the critic ought to justify the presence of extraneous matter in the poem or admit that the author bungled badly. Critics have long ignored such basic obligations as the necessity of accounting for all parts of the poem.

The burlesque-satire approach can embrace every portion of the birds' squabble because any issue the birds raise is *ipso facto* part of their quarrel and hence relevant to a satire on contentiousness. Even more significantly, this approach can account for the peculiar yoking of serious issues (like adultery) and the avian protagonists, a combination which damages many another interpretation, for the birds are incontrovertibly silly. We see them falling all over themselves to pounce on argumentative points, only to lose sight of their objective and wander off without pinning the opposition down. Time and again one or the other seems to be on the verge of making a telling point but fails for want of the most elementary intelligence. When screeching insults over diet, they are not much different from two real birds, frantically squawking and tugging from both ends of a worm. Such birds – and our protagonists – so lack dignity that they are hardly appropriate as serious representatives of mankind. Yet they mention issues of considerable importance to man. Such incompatibility between avian vehicle and some of the subjects is entirely appropriate to a burlesque-satire reading. Indeed, burlesque is defined by the presence of just such an incongruity: it is a ridiculing through *incongruous* imitation. The birds imitate man in his concern for these weighty issues, and naturally fail to handle them appropriately.

Another way of describing burlesque is to look at the act of mind behind its genesis. Burlesque may result if an artist perceives that some person, institution, practice, or idea is overvalued. His response is an attempt to deflate the overrated object by creating a comically distorted imitation, an imitation which exaggerates the weaknesses, thus bringing them to our attention. He operates like a caricaturist, enlarging the already prominent nose or reducing still further the negligible chin. The butt of *The Owl and the Nightingale* is human quarrelling, which we overrate by respecting it and taking it seriously, often investing it with solemn legal or intellectual trappings. The weaknesses to be exaggerated are quarrelling's ineffectuality and destructiveness, perhaps even the false sense of importance it engenders in the contestants. The Owl and Nightingale are exactly suited for this job of deflation. Many animals could fill the post adequately, but these two are particularly successful because of their colourful personalities. Were two stones to debate, the result would probably be soporific. The folk, literary, and religious lore adhering to these birds gives them all sorts of dimensions of character and contributes many interests to their arguments. The unusual, conflicting nature of the traditions regarding both birds is responsible for a great enrichment of the poem, more indeed than we tend to be aware of unless we try to visualize other animals or other types of speakers such as stones, flowers, or rivers. The funny, contradictory nature of the birds is central both to the favourable impression the poem makes on us and to its overall satiric mission.

The Owl and the Nightingale is a poem in which many forces and many forms come together in felicitous concert. One on top of the other, we find poetic debate, beast fable, begging poem, and satire on sin, the result better by far than most examples of any one form because richer. The poem catches and entertains the mind because of the complex congruences of these various forms. The forces are equally intriguing: moral exhortation, presented in so whimsical and charming a fashion as to be utterly disarming. Nothing more turns our sympathies off than a bungled pleading poem – whining self-pity, greed, and improper ambition are likely to irritate the listener, as happens in some of Dunbar's pleas. Nicholas keeps his plea light, pleasing us with the glittering web of the whole, into which is woven the supplication. As a result we are inclined to wish his cause well. The moderation, both in entreaty and in moral fervour, strike a modern audience particularly favourably. When viewed amidst other medieval poems, this one radiates an unusually humane attitude towards life. The author sees the birds' essential silliness, and does not gloss over their nastiness. Yet he also lets us see occasional flashes of bravery, occasional kindly impulses – towards man if not each other. We enjoy their boundless vigour, and like them despite their faults. We come to feel sharply the pathos of their deaths: the little Nightingale drawn apart by wild horses for 'treachery,' the Owl stoned – by children even – and hung on a rod, both for trivial misunderstandings. The author's ability to see the pain in those two unimportant deaths sets his work far apart from the more usual stylized treatments of animals in equivalent poems. The stoning of a hundred cuckoos like the fairly attractive cynic in *The Cuckoo and the Nightingale*, and the love anguish of a thousand nightingales is not to be compared to the killing of our two. They are incomparably more real, more 'realized' for us by the poet, and his work is the greater for arousing such a response.

If we can abandon futile desires to find an *issue* in or allegorically behind the poem, and simply accept the subject as it is given to us, then the poem can be judged an imaginative triumph. The author makes us vividly aware of the nasty futility of the sort of aimless squabbling most people accept and carry on as a matter of course. The poem lets us see just how foolish we can look. The *speculum* or mirror held up with corrective and instructive intention was an image much loved in the Middle Ages. The birds are a kind of mirror – a comically distorting mirror with odd bulges and tricks to clothe the actors' antic forms in feathers. Yet rare is the honest beholder who cannot see himself amidst skirmishes like this. The birds invite such identification. After all, in one of the poem's most graceful ironies, the original reader was asked to align himself with them and agree that Nicholas should be given preferment.

NOTES

1 See Ernst Robert Curtius, *European Literature and the Latin Middle Ages*, trans. Willard R. Trask (orig. German, 1948; translation, New York: Harper and Row 1963) 83–5, for *topoi* to express 'affected modesty.'
2 Lines 235, 294, 299, 349, 569, 685, 697, 761, 942, 1074, 1223, and 1269

index of lines cited and alluded to directly

index